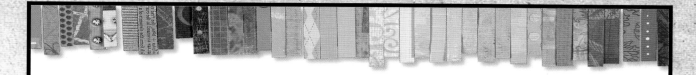

Playing with Paper

Innovative Ideas for Using Patterned Papers in Your Scrapbooks

Angelia Wigginton

MEMORY
MAKERS
BOOKS

CINCINNATI, OHIO
WWW.MYCRAFTIVITY.COM

Playing with Paper. Copyright© 2009 by Angelia Wigginton. Manufactured in China. All rights
reserved. It is permissible for the purchaser to make the projects contained herein and sell them
at fairs, bazaars and craft shows. No other part of this book may be reproduced in any form or by
any electronic or mechanical means including information storage and retrieval systems without
permission in writing from the publisher, except by a reviewer, who may quote a brief passage in
review. Published by Memory Makers Books, an imprint of F+W Media, Inc., 4700 East Galbraith
Road, Cincinnati, Ohio 45236. (800) 289-0963. First edition.

13 12 11 10 09   5 4 3 2 1

Distributed in Canada by Fraser Direct
100 Armstrong Avenue
Georgetown, ON, Canada L7G 5S4
Tel: (905) 877-4411

Distributed in the U.K. and Europe by David & Charles
Brunel House, Newton Abbot, Devon, TQ12 4PU, England
Tel: (+44) 1626 323200, Fax: (+44) 1626 323319
E-mail: postmaster@davidandcharles.co.uk

Distributed in Australia by Capricorn Link
P.O. Box 704, S. Windsor, NSW 2756 Australia
Tel: (02) 4577-3555

Library of Congress Cataloging-in-Publication Data

Wigginton, Angelia.
  Playing with paper : innovative ideas for using patterned
  papers in your scrapbooks / Angelia Wigginton. -- 1st ed.
    p. cm.
  Includes bibliographical references and index.
  ISBN 978-1-59963-033-5 (pbk. : alk. paper)
  1. Paper work. 2. Scrapbooking. I. Memory Makers Books (Firm) II. Title.
  TT870.W53 2009
  745.593--dc22

                    2008034953

Editor: Kristin Boys
Designer: Steven Peters
Art Coordinator: Eileen Aber
Production Coordinator: Greg Nock
Photographers: Ric Deliantoni, Adam Hand
Stylist: Lauren Emmerling

www.fwmedia.com

Metric Conversion Chart

to convert	to	multiply by
Inches	Centimeters	2.54
Centimeters	Inches	0.4
Feet	Centimeters	30.5
Centimeters	Feet	0.03
Yards	Meters	0.9
Meters	Yards	1.1
Sq. Inches	Sq. Centimeters	6.45
Sq. Centimeters	Sq. Inches	0.16
Sq. Feet	Sq. Meters	0.09
Sq. Meters	Sq. Feet	10.8
Sq. Yards	Sq. Meters	0.8
Sq. Meters	Sq. Yards	1.2
Pounds	Kilograms	0.45
Kilograms	Pounds	2.2
Ounces	Grams	28.3
Grams	Ounces	0.035

About the Author

Angelia Wigginton lives in Belmont,
Mississippi, with her husband, Rich, their
two daughters, Olivia and Michaela, and a
trio of cats. She began scrapbooking eight
years ago, after discovering scrapbooking
supplies at a local flea market. Since that
time her love for all things related
to scrapbooking and papercrafting
has only grown deeper. As a
computer engineer turned stay-at-
home mom, she has devoted many
hours to this hobby. She describes
her style as "linear, clean, and
colorful." Angelia loves patterned
papers, buttons, brads and rub-
ons, and delights in finding just
the right color scheme or pattern
combo to "set the mood" for her
photos and stories.

The top 2 photos - very, very you, 80% of the time.
The middle photo - for all of 1% of the time.
The bottom photo - silly for the remainder 19%.
You love each other 100%,
but you try hard not to show it!

Olivia and Michaela, Christmas Eve, 2007

Dedication

I dedicate this book to my mom, Maedean Allen. Thank you for always believing in me, for your example of faith and courage, and for being my best friend.

Acknowledgments

When I began scrapbooking in the summer of 1998, I would never have dreamed that 10 years later, not only would I still be scrapbooking, but I'd be writing a book on the subject. Who knew that a brief stop at a scrapbooking booth in a local flea market would turn into what my husband calls my obsession? I do know that this hobby reached into my heart, found a comfy spot and made a home.

My heartfelt thanks goes to:

My dearest husband, Rich, for putting up with all the uncooked meals and piles (and piles) of scrapbooking stuff, and for his unwavering love and support in all that I do.

My girls, Olivia and Michaela, for being the never-ending joy in my life.

My editors, Christine Doyle and Kristin Boys, for their confidence and support, and for turning my very rough draft into a real book.

My team—Susan Weinroth, Amber Baley, Irma Gabbard, Jennifer Gallacher, Linda Albrecht, Jennifer Olson, Nicole Samuels, Greta Hammond, Kelly Purkey, Davinie Fiero, Cari Locken, Lisa Storms, Christine Drumheller and Mary MacAskill—for the honor and pleasure of working with such talented scrapbookers. Without their help, I could not have completed this book.

K&Company, Fancy Pants Designs, Scenic Route Paper Company, 7Gypsies and Me & My Big Ideas for supporting me with their generous donations of product.

Contents

YUM

Michaela, 6

Marissa, 5

simple thi

Famil

The five of you are very different.
Each is unique.
But, together, you are family, and
a trip to the pumpkin patch with family
is so much more fun than going alone.

endless Possibilities

2 girls

Boys are precious, too. I should
know. I've got 4 nephews. But,
I've always been happy with
having 2 girls. And although you
have the normal fusses and
fights that sisters will be

Roxy

pond

I remember this po
amazed by it, and u
turning in the mirror

I remember this dre
your eyes pop, and t
sweetest blanket stitc
along the rick rack w

But, you being two seems c

You still like ponytails, bu
a simple barrette on the
rather be wearing a Han
t-shirt and shorts.

2007

Visiting the aquarium in Vancouver, B.C.   over spring break was such an   amazing experience! It had   been a long while since

I'd been to a major aquarium.   We spent the entire   day 'oohing and aaahhing' over the unique   marine life. Being there and taking it all in

was definitely

seeing the aquatic world   in LIVING color

I fell in love with this city... hard. There are so many things about Chicago that make me happy: the places, people, food. The one place I feel truly at home. I am so lucky to live in this amazing city!

forever and e

I LOVE YOU, chicago.

Who Can Resist?

Some of my fondest memories are of nights spent at my grandparents' house. My grandmother had a brass bed with a feather mattress that, for a little girl, seemed a mile high. At bedtime, she would cover us with one or two of her handmade quilts. These quilts were made with many small pieces of patterned fabric in a wide range of colors, and I remember loving them. The colorful mix-and-match of the patterns dancing across the quilt made me feel happy. Patterned papers have the same effect on me, although they don't keep me as warm! I just can't resist the florals, stripes, dots and geometrics in every color of the rainbow. Patterned paper is my all-time favorite scrapbook supply. You can't beat it for beauty, versatility and all-out fun. I tell my husband that I must have lots on hand because "you never know"! (I don't think he's buying that explanation, though.)

Like me, you probably can't resist all the paper sitting on store shelves. But has all that paper made its way onto your scrapbook pages? This book is designed to take the mystery out of adding a little pattern into your life, one chapter at a time. You won't find "don't do this" or "this is the wrong way" or "that is a no-no" in this book. Instead, look for easy techniques and simple "try this" tips on using patterned paper to enhance your photos and stories. Instead of feeling overwhelmed by all the wonderful paper choices you have, you can work with smaller pieces, create a jazzy title or weave an easy accent block.

Using patterned paper isn't like cleaning your plate at the supper table. I'm giving you permission to take it slow, to start with a little and to save the rest for later. I encourage you to experiment and play. I have a feeling you will get hooked on patterned paper … and, despite what my husband might say, it isn't such a bad thing!

{celebratiNg 12}

What they say is true.

Time flies.

I remember the first time

I saw your face.

I remember all the

birthdays in between.

I'm not ready

for a teenager.

Love, Momma.

beautiful

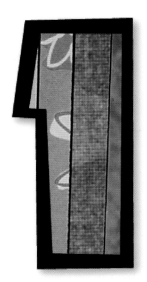

A Little Goes a Long Way
Using one or two patterned papers

Before diving into the deep end (lots of patterned paper floating around there!), start right here. Take it slowly and get a little experience incorporating one or two patterns into your scrapbook layouts. And remember—a few patterns can still add up to exciting pages.

The first step in choosing patterned papers for a layout is to have an idea of what you want your scrapbook page to communicate. How do you want readers to feel when they look at your page? What type of story are you telling? What patterns and colors will help you enhance the moments in your photos? As you look at the examples in this chapter, take special notice of how the paper choices bring out the story on the layout, and how just a little print can go a long way toward making a great page.

Bookend Photos

Michaela couldn't wait to zoom down the hill on her new bike! After studying the photos, I chose two patterns in the same hues as my photos. Plus, the circle print reflected the shape of a bicycle wheel. I highlighted the series of photos by creating "bookends" with my papers. To copy this look, mat your focal photo on one side with cardstock, and then add patterned papers behind the cardstock. Repeat this on the other side matching the height of the background paper on the left.

Supplies: Cardstock (Bazzill); patterned paper (BasicGrey, Fontwerks); letter stickers (Arctic Frog, Me & My Big Ideas); die-cut flower (Scenic Route); brads, chipboard hearts (Making Memories); acrylic accent (Heidi Swapp); decorative punches (EK Success); Misc: Corbel font

A Slice of Life

Pumpkin carving can get a little messy, but it sure makes for a good time. I wanted my layout to reflect the fun of our evening. This ivory lined paper allows my busier photos to be the focus, and the printed lines work well for adding journaling. Experiment with different colors to find the most pleasing background color for your photos. Then crop your photos into "slices," and frame your collage of photos with narrow strips of paper. Just a little of this orange-and-green stripe did the "trick" for me.

Supplies: Cardstock (Bazzill); patterned paper (Creative Imaginations, Scenic Route); letter stickers (American Crafts, BasicGrey); rub-ons (BasicGrey); glitter chipboard, rhinestones (K&Co.); die-cut shapes (Scenic Route); Misc: 2Peas Evergreen font

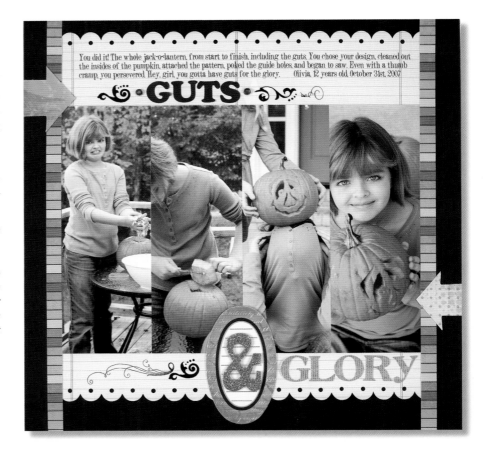

While cruisin' to Mexico, we had a rain shower. This was the perfect opportunity to get the girls out of the pool (they love swimming), and to check out some of the other amenities the ship offered. Out on deck it was a bit wet, but that didn't stop Rich and Olivia from playing a game of ping pong. It just meant that they got a little wet if they had to chase the ball very far. Before long, the rain stopped and we could see land in the distance. The girls packed their backpacks and watched the land grow nearer. They were ready for an on-shore adventure! Summer, 2005

Strip of Ocean

While on a cruise, we didn't let a little rain spoil our fun. We just moved to the ping pong table under the covered deck. I wanted to play up the blues in these photos, so I chose a subtle blue pattern for my background. The crisp white of the journaling box and the alphabet stickers represents the little white ball from our game. To add a bit of pizzazz to your own page with a subtle background, add colorful strips of patterned paper along the top and bottom of your layout.

Supplies: Cardstock (Bazzill); patterned paper (BasicGrey, KI Memories); letter stickers (American Crafts); metal accent (K&Co.); Misc: 2Peas Evergreen font

Sunblock

When looking at these photos, I'm reminded of our summer afternoon at the park. The sun was shining, and boy, was it hot! I wanted to create a "hot summer" feel for this layout, so I took my cues from the color of my kids' T-shirts. Just a block of orange pattern and a block of lime green allows these park photos to really shine. To contrast bright colors, just add some black details and make a page pop.

Supplies: Cardstock (Bazzill, Prism); patterned paper (Me & My Big Ideas); chipboard letters, letter stickers (American Crafts); rub-on (Dèjá Views); acrylic tag, brads (Making Memories); Misc: Century Gothic Bold font

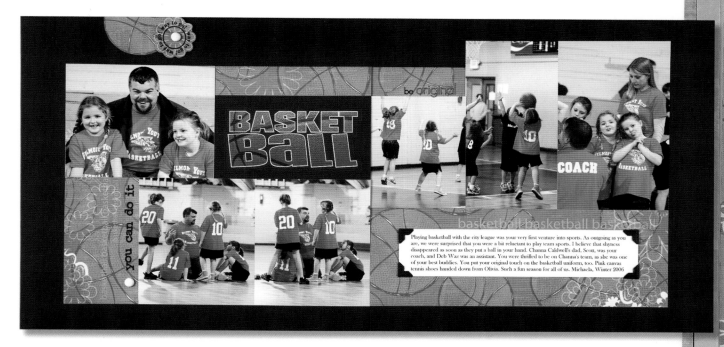

Making the Most of It

Michaela's basketball team loved playing together, and you couldn't miss them coming in those orange uniforms. I found the perfect themed print for these photos, but I had only one sheet. So I set out to make the most of it. To complete this look, begin by arranging your photos on two sheets of cardstock in colors that complement your photos. Fill the "holes" with blocks of your patterned paper.

Supplies: Cardstock (Bazzill); patterned paper (Reminisce); rub-on title (Scrappin' Sports); rub-ons (Scenic Route); photo corners (Canson); Misc: Baskerville Old Face font

Be Square

Beach photos are some of my favorites to scrapbook. With sunny pictures full of color, I often choose just one pattern and apply it in small quantities. The grid design here allows for lots of photos, and the pattern adds visual interest without distracting from the focus of the page. Cutting the photos and patterned paper squares to 3" × 3" (8cm × 8cm) leaves room for a solid cardstock border all around.

Supplies: Cardstock (Bazzill); patterned paper (Me & My Big Ideas); letter stickers (Doodlebug, KI Memories); chipboard letters (American Crafts); chipboard tag, plastic letters (Heidi Swapp); rub-ons (Dèjà Views, Die Cuts With A View, Scenic Route); photo turn (7gypsies); brads (Making Memories); Misc: Arial Black font

Tone It Down

It's never too early to learn to love books, as Mary's little one already knows. Mary chose a color scheme of neutrals and a soft green to complement the important elements in her photos (the baby and her book). She reinforced her book theme by using a patterned paper block with tone-on-tone alphabet characters. To highlight your own focal photo and title treatment, create a "bookshelf" across your layout with a horizontal journaling block.

Supplies: Cardstock (Bazzill, My Mind's Eye); patterned paper (Daisy D's, Scenic Route); paper trim (Doodlebug); rhinestones, stamp (Hero Arts); buttons, sticker accents (American Crafts); silhouette word (Heidi Swapp); Misc: Suede font, stamping ink

Artwork by Mary MacAskill

The photo layout reads:

{celebratiNg 12}

What they say is true.
Time flies.
I remember the first time
I saw your face.
I remember all the
birthdays in between.
I'm not ready
for a teenager.
Love, Momma.

beautiful

Bigger Is Better

These playful photos of my daughter reminded me that she would soon be a teenager, and I wanted to create a page about my thoughts on the matter. Here, I chose a print with paint-spattered details as my background and balanced that artsy look with classic black-and-white photos. I also used embellishments in the same color family as my paper to create a subtle—rather than bright and bold—design. On your own page, stick with one large accent to keep a layout with a printed background from looking too busy.

Supplies: Cardstock; die-cut butterfly, patterned paper (Fancy Pants); glitter numbers (K&Co.); brackets (American Crafts); rub-on letters (Daisy D's); flower (Prima); brads (KI Memories, Making Memories); buttons (Autumn Leaves); rhinestones (Me & My Big Ideas)

Paper Chase

If you're going to play with paper, you have to start with paper! Here's a short guide to the kinds you'll find.

- **Cardstock.** While solid cardstock, by definition, doesn't have a pattern, it can be just as essential to a page. Solid cardstock balances out busy prints, and stocking up on neutral shades ensures you always have a color that matches.
- **Heavy-Weight Patterned Paper.** When you need a sturdy background sheet but you want more pattern and color than solid cardstock can provide, heavy-weight patterned paper is the way to go.
- **Double-Sided Patterned Paper.** Get more bang for your buck! With two sides, you have twice as many options, and you're guaranteed to have at least two patterns that coordinate perfectly.
- **Digital Patterned Paper.** Of course, digital patterned paper will help you create gorgeous digital layouts. But print out a paper and you've got a great option for creating hand-cut paper details, too.

Give Me a Ring

Looking at these photos makes me laugh. It might look like a hug, but I think Olivia is really thinking about choking Michaela instead. For this humorous layout about having a little sister, I chose a whimsical print with swirls, stars, circles and flowers. To add detail and dimension, and a visual triangle of movement, I covered chipboard circles and rings with a pattern, a technique you can learn below. Die-cut rings and buttons add some fun.

Supplies: Cardstock (Bazzill); die-cut shapes, patterned paper (Fancy Pants); letter stickers (Making Memories); chipboard shapes (Bazzill, Fancy Pants); buttons (Doodlebug); Misc: Cooper Black font

March 4th, 2006

Olivia says sisters are
always in my room
too loud
in the way
unnecessary
following me around
annoying
taking my things

Momma says
NOT

Play with it!

Dress Chipboard with Paper

Materials: chipboard, paper, liquid adhesive, craft knife, craft mat, sanding tool or ink

Apply a thin coat of liquid adhesive to the front of your chipboard piece. Place it facedown onto the back side of the patterned paper. Allow the adhesive to dry.

Place the chipboard on the craft mat and trim off the excess paper using the craft knife.

For added detail, sand the edges with a file or sanding sponge, as shown, or add ink to the chipboard edges.

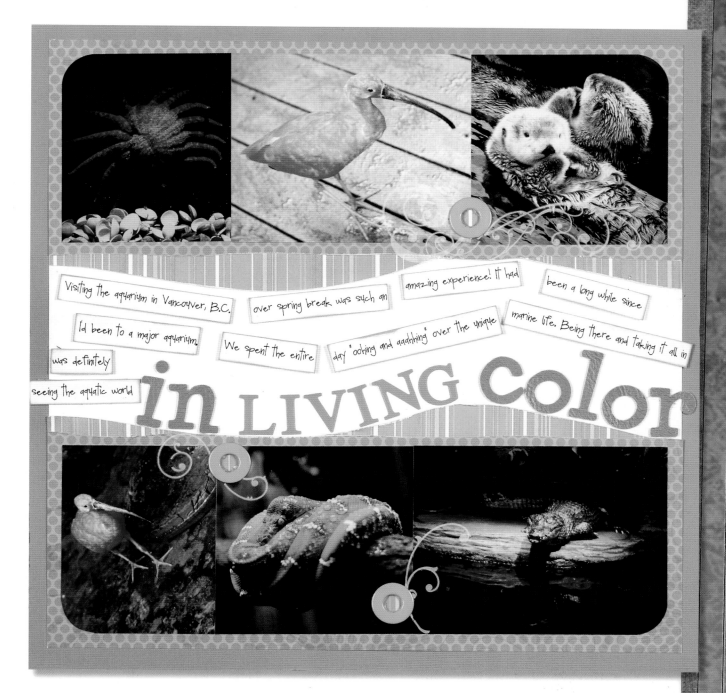

Visiting the aquarium in Vancouver, B.C. over spring break was such an amazing experience! It had been a long while since I'd been to a major aquarium. We spent the entire day "oohing and aaahhing" over the unique marine life. Being there and taking it all in was definitely seeing the aquatic world **in LIVING color**

Doing the Wave

Zoos are full of action, excitement, color and motion, and Jenn created the perfect page to show off just that, with vivid colors and hints of movement. Her monochromatic green background highlights the colors in the photos. The striped pattern cut in wavy lines creates a sense of motion. Take a cue from Jenn and enhance curves by creating waves with your title and journaling.

Supplies: Cardstock (Bazzill); patterned paper (Scenic Route); letter stickers (American Crafts, Collage Press); Misc: FG Jasmine font

Artwork by Jenn Olson

Border Patrol

During the Christmas holidays in 2002, my mom used lots of gold decorations in her home, and the result was beautiful. I began this page with a gallery of photos taken in her living room, knowing I wanted sparkle and detail to highlight the photos. This patterned paper gave me an easy start, with a detailed border built right in. All I had to do was add some shiny, glittery embellishments. It goes to show that when shopping for patterns, you should be on the lookout for pre-printed border designs that can be used to easily add details.

Supplies: Cardstock (Prism); adhesive rub-ons, flowers, glitter, patterned paper, rhinestones (K&Co.); glitter chipboard (Making Memories); rub-on title (Dèjá Views); acrylic accent (Heidi Swapp); Misc: 2Peas Evergreen font

Clearly a Great Idea

My nephews are a hoot—this is what you get when you try to make them sit still for a few minutes. Paper designs with silly frogs and big green polka dots say "little boy" to me, so I added just a touch of these patterns to the solid background. Patterned paper makes for a great title. To use it effectively, add a block of one print to the background, and attach transparent title letters over the top. Cut a detail—like my frog—to place over a letter.

Supplies: Cardstock (Bazzill); patterned paper (BasicGrey, Creative Imaginations); acrylic letters (Heidi Swapp); letter stickers (American Crafts, K&Co.); rub-ons (Urban Lily); brads, chipboard stars (Making Memories); glitter brads (Doodlebug); Misc: 2Peas Tiny Tadpole font

Make a Photo Sandwich

Davinie's baby girl photos take center stage on this page with only one patterned paper. Her page says soft and sweet with its scalloped borders, machine stitching and gingham ribbon. These details are fabulous, and the framing technique really sets this page apart. She used pre-made chipboard coasters in a cute print to sandwich her photo block. Follow Davinie's example to balance your busier embellishments: Pair them with a classic print like polka dots or a tone-on-tone pattern.

Supplies: Cardstock (Bazzill); brads, patterned paper, ribbon (Making Memories); chipboard flower, letter stickers (American Crafts); cherry rhinestone (Heidi Swapp); label stickers (Fontwerks, Making Memories); vintage cherry coaster (Studio Calico); paper punch (Marvy)

Artwork by Davinie Fiero

Stick with the Classics

Michaela would spend all her money on stuffed animals if I let her. With black-and-white photos, you can easily choose a color scheme that suits your theme. For my page all about bunnies and love, I stuck with a classic mix: pink, red and black. To begin your page, cut a piece of scalloped cardstock in half and add that to your background. Then place a vertical striped print on the bottom of the page to draw the eye down to the photos. For a little added interest, use a decorative-edge paper like the bracket-shaped paper I used.

Supplies: Cardstock (Bazzill); brads, glitter chipboard, patterned paper (Making Memories); letter stickers (American Crafts); chipboard letters (Heidi Swapp); rub-ons (BasicGrey); chipboard hearts and tag (Me & My Big Ideas); rhinestone heart (K&Co.); ribbon (May Arts); Misc: Times New Roman font, chipboard scrolls

Balancing Act

I don't have many photos of myself with my girls, so I treasure the few that I have (thank you, Janet!). This page shows you can balance two strong patterns successfully. Incorporating red into both halves of the page allows the patterns to complement each other. The feminine white-and-ivory print, although busy, with its single color acts as a place to rest against the bolder pattern created by the numbers. The simplicity of the photo and the journaling block allows them to shine against the background.

Supplies: Cardstock (Bazzill); die-cut cardstock (KI Memories); glitter letters, patterned paper (Making Memories); chipboard bracket (Fancy Pants); rhinestones (Heidi Swapp); rub-on (Dèjá Views); photo corner (K&Co.); Misc: 2Peas Evergreen font (Photo by Janet Dominick)

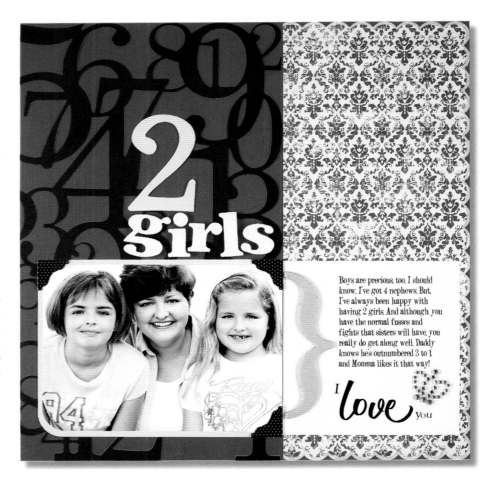

At 10 years old, you still liked pink, and you LOVED the beach. You rode this multi-color board over and over, despite getting dumped. You would spit the saltwater out of your mouth, swipe your face, and be ready for the next wave. I was envious of your energy AND your tan, but having too much fun with you to notice it much!

sweeter than sugar

All that Glitters

I know you've seen them—those gorgeous embossed, glittered patterns with bold, graphic designs. But how do you use them on a scrapbook page? Keep it simple! When working with a bold pattern that also has added detail (like glitter) mix it with a solid cardstock and keep additional elements to a minimum. It also helps to use simple shapes, like my rounded-corner rectangles. The balance allows the beauty of the pattern to shine through without taking anything away from your photos or story.

Supplies: Cardstock (Bazzill); patterned paper (K&Co., Sassafras Lass); letter stickers (American Crafts); felt word (K&Co.); buttons (Doodlebug); paper punch (EK Success); rub-on (BasicGrey); Misc: Arial font

Less Is More

Jenn captured this funky photo of a street band while traveling. Playing off the black and gray tones in the photo, she chose a full sheet of gray patterned paper as her background. Jenn shows that even if you use only one pattern, your page can be far from plain. On this layout, brightly colored accents draw the eye in, balance the busy background print and highlight the photo.

Supplies: Cardstock (Bazzill); patterned paper (Making Memories); paper trim (Doodlebug); letter stickers (American Crafts, Heidi Swapp); labels (Fontwerks, Heidi Swapp)

Artwork by Jenn Olson

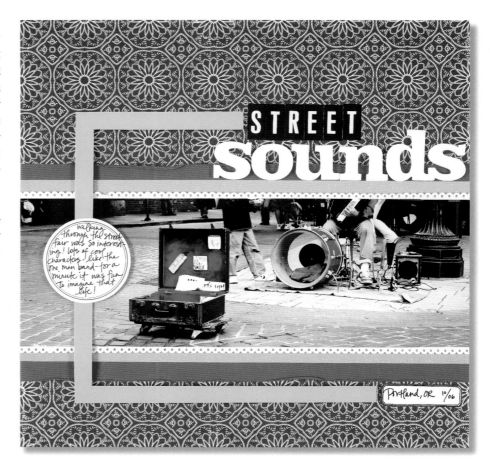

Finishing Touch

Susan snaps photos of all the little details that catch her eye while on vacation. A collage of these images is perfect for prompting memories, and it needs only a bit of pattern for some extra spunk. Accent a group of your own photos by choosing a solid cardstock background and then adding a strip of patterned paper along the base of the photos for a finishing touch.

Supplies: Cardstock (Bazzill); chipboard stickers, patterned paper, rub-ons (Heidi Grace); letter stickers (American Crafts); paper punches (Fiskars); Misc: IC American Typewriter font

Artwork by Susan Weinwroth

These four cousins love riding on Poppa Pat's pontoon boat. Yes, it is a bit noisy and a bit crowded when we all pile on, but it's also a lot of fun. Before long, the kids begin asking "when can we stop and play on the beach?" They are happy with any patch of sand along the lake, and will play for hours, or until they get hungry!

Evan, 6, Olivia, 5, Austin, 4, Michaela, 18 months

July 2001

fun
4
x

Blues Cues

These photos of my girls and nephews playing on the beach are great examples of how photos can provide pattern cues. To re-create this design, begin with a neutral background (I used a sandy color). Choose a pattern that repeats a design found in your photos, like the blue leafy print here, which is similar to my nephews' shorts and supports the summer theme. Place a wide strip of that pattern, balanced by a wide area for your journaling and title, on the page. To finish, add a simple print (like dots) in small strips to frame a photo collage.

Supplies: Cardstock (Bazzill); patterned paper (Me & My Big Ideas, Scenic Route); chipboard number (Zsiage); chipboard exclamation point, letter stickers (American Crafts); brads, chipboard hearts (Making Memories); Misc: Cooper Black font

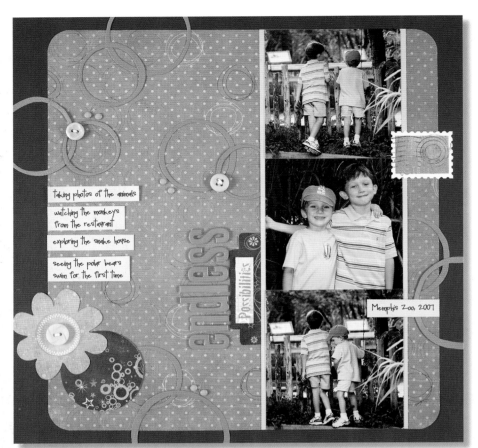

Never Say Never

I think these two tried to cover every inch of the zoo, which made for lots of great photos to choose from. When photos have a lot going on, like mine do, it's not impossible to pair them with a background pattern. Just be sure to choose a subtle print, like this dotted one, in a color that highlights those in your photos. Then incorporate a second pattern in small doses, like I did with my embellishments. Use solid colors for additional details, like my journaling strips, photo mats and circles that mimic that background pattern.

Supplies: Cardstock (Bazzill); die-cut shapes, patterned paper (Fancy Pants); chipboard letters (Heidi Swapp); brads (Making Memories); buttons (Autumn Leaves); circle punch (Provo Craft); Misc: Peas Lacy font (Photos by Cindy Howell)

Shape Up

Lisa's page is a perfect example of so easy, yet so fabulous! Although her layout features baseball shots of her son, I can envision this technique looking cool with a variety of photos, papers and shapes. To re-create this technique, cut circles or other shapes in various sizes out of your background pattern. Ink the shapes, rotate them and then reattach them to the background. Add a title treatment and journaling to one of the larger shapes to complete the look.

Supplies: Cardstock (Bazzill); patterned paper (Cloud 9); chipboard letters (Heidi Grace); Misc: Soli font, twine

Artwork by Lisa Storms

make the most of it

Twelve. You've reached that in between age. Not a child, and not a teenager. As I watch you struggle, with responsibilities at home, schoolwork, and relating to others, I just want to give you the biggest hug. I want to tell you that everything will work out. Most of all, I want to say "I love you" and "I'm proud of you". I wish I could save you the frustrations, the fears, and the failures. I can't. Instead, I will encourage you thru the hard times, and help you celebrate the victories. I will always be here for you. I hope you will look on the bright side and do your best in all things. Love yourself for all the good things you are, for all the good things you do, and for just being Evan. With all my love, Aunt Angie. Photos, August 2007. Journaling, January 2008.

enjoy

Simply Say It

I can't believe my oldest nephew is almost a teenager! I created this journaling-focused layout to offer him some advice and encouragement. Since the words are the focus, I didn't need a lot of pattern detail, just two simple papers. I chose distressed patterns of blue and green to complement the snapshots taken near the water. To get a similar look, simply use one paper color as your background, then cut a panel of the other paper color, distress the outer edge for added detail and attach it to the background.

Supplies: Patterned paper (BasicGrey); rub-ons (BasicGrey, Scenic Route, Urban Lily); brads (Doodlebug); Misc: Arial font

3-way Three photos, three ways

Here, three different artists use the same three photos (above) on a layout. These layouts show that there are a number of ways to enhance photos using one or two patterns on a page.

Bright and Balanced

I wanted to mimic the feeling of the relaxing boat ride on a hot summer day shown in the photos, so I chose patterns in hot summer shades of lime green and orange and accented them with sunshine yellow. For added texture, I machine-stitched waves to a panel of patterned paper. I used scraps of patterned paper to create "suns" and added button centers. Finally, I attached alphabet stickers around my embellishments to add a sense of movement to the design.

Supplies: Cardstock (Bazzill); patterned paper (Autumn Leaves, Fancy Pants); letter stickers (American Crafts); rub-ons (BasicGrey, Die Cuts With A View); photo turn (7gypsies); brads (Making Memories); Misc: 2Peas Favorite Things font, buttons

Cool and Complementary

As I did, Jennifer used an enlargement to highlight the focal photo. But Jennifer added just a bit of patterned paper in aqua to both complement and cool down all the orange in the photos. She also used the second print just for accents (in the form of clouds) so as not to overwhelm the page. The solid cardstock anchors the patterns and bright colors.

Supplies: Cardstock (Bazzill, Prism); patterned paper (KI Memories); chipboard letters (Scenic Route); photo corners (Canson); button, flower (American Crafts); floss (Karen Foster); leaf (Making Memories); paper punches (Marvy, unknown); decorative scissors (Provo Craft); Misc: Batik Regular font

Artwork by Jennifer Gallacher

Although, Michaela had ridden in Grandpa's pontoon before, she didn't remember it so it felt like the first time all over again. She was so excited that she didn't even complain about wearing the life jacket. At the end of the day she cooled off by finishing off her own drink and then starting in on mine.

Subtle and Simple

Irma took an entirely different approach with her photos. To highlight the focal point, she simply placed it in the center of the trio of pictures. The tone-on-tone orange look—created by the bright orange in the photos and the solid cardstock background—creates a sunny but subtle look for the page. Like Jennifer and me, she used paper to create embellishments, although hers are solid colored. She brought in pattern with a thin, brightly colored strip that works to balance the photos' bright hues at the top of the page.

Supplies: Cardstock (Bazzill); patterned paper (Provo Craft); chipboard accents (Scenic Route); brads (Doodlebug); Misc: 2Peas Plain Jane font

Artwork by Irma Gabbard

PLAYFUL

SPLASH

the BEST part of our trip was...
watching Michaela enjoy herself on the boat.
She was just so happy to sit in the boat and drink
my Mt. Dew and watch everyone else go on the innertube.

NEW YORK

check out that

view

the view from Liberty Island
was so amazing. It was great
to see the lower Manhattan
skyline from a different
angle. I couldn't resist popping
a quarter into the viewfinder
and taking a closer peek. How
can such a big city look so
small?

The Power of Three

Mixing three patterned papers

Three is one of those magical numbers that pops up in fairytales, stories, myths and even in design. There is some special power in that number—threes always seems to work. And working with three patterned papers is no exception.

If you're at a loss as to where to start, choose a striped print, a print with small simple details and an "almost solid" (a print that looks like a solid from a distance). My layout "Game On" on page 30 is a great example of how well this easy combination works on a layout. Even if you use this technique for every one of your layouts, all your pages can still have totally different looks. Play around with how much and where you put patterns on the page. Use three blocks of prints. Or use one pattern as your background, and the other two papers as your embellishments or border treatments. Don't forget to have fun! Eventually you'll be on your way to branching out and trying three patterns in all kinds of ways. Whatever you choose, using three patterns allows you a lot of freedom with your design.

Start Simple

After playing Sorry! on our vacation cruise, the girls asked to purchase the game to play at home. (I think they get their competitive streak from their dad.) After studying these photos, I knew I wanted to use colors similar to the gameboard, and I found the perfect pattern of multicolored stripes. To tone down that bold print, I chose two simpler patterns: a subtle orange print with small numbers and an "almost" solid brown dot pattern. If you look closely, you'll see I created a panel design, which complements the graphic look of the patterns.

Supplies: Cardstock (Bazzill); patterned paper (KI Memories); letter stickers (American Crafts, Arctic Frog); chipboard accent (Urban Lily); rub-ons (Scenic Route); Misc: Arial Black font

Neutral Base

I had to beg. "Just five," I asked sweetly, before resorting to bribery. It was worth it. The journaling on this one will be the kind of thing they will enjoy reading years from now. To complement this gorgeous photo, I combined two coordinating prints, a stripe and a floral, with a decorative-edged ledger print. These three prints work together because the colors in each are similar and have a neutral base. Plus, the busier flower pattern is balanced by the subtler stripe and ledger prints.

Supplies: Cardstock (Bazzill); patterned paper (BasicGrey, Making Memories); chipboard letters (American Crafts, Scenic Route); rub-ons (Autumn Leaves, BasicGrey, Li'l Davis); transparent accent (Creative Imaginations); Misc: Times New Roman font

I'm thankful for you, Michaela. I'm thankful for the time we spend together, and our annual trip to the pumpkin farm. I'm thankful for 15 minutes to take photos of you before you scamper off to explore the farm. I'm thankful that you delight in being outdoors and that you appreciate the beauty that God has created all around us.

thankful

4

Gridlock

I love scrapping pumpkin patch photos, so for this page I chose three of my favorites and shared some of my feelings about this time of year. This layout shows how you can use patterns in unexpected ways. I used a block of neutral-colored grid as my main pattern for the page; the subtle grid locks in a solid design and allows the words to be the focus. The other two patterns—a pumpkin-colored floral and a red dotted print—make sweet and simple embellishments. Both prints add just the punch of the color the mostly neutral page needs.

Supplies: Cardstock (Bazzill); patterned paper (Chatterbox); rub-ons (BasicGrey, Dèjá Views); chipboard number (American Crafts); brads (Creative Imaginations); photo turn (7gypsies); wooden frame (Li'l Davis); Misc: Times New Roman font, buttons

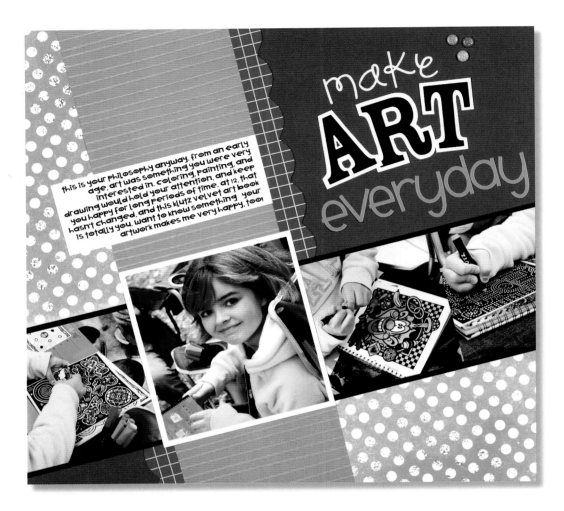

this is your philosophy anyway. from an early age, art was something you were very interested in. coloring, painting, and drawing would hold your attention, and keep you happy for long periods of time. at 12, that hasn't changed, and this klutz velvet art book is totally you. want to know something? your artwork makes me very happy, too!

make ART everyday

Playful Placement

This Klutz Velvet Art book was worth every penny. I drew inspiration for my color choices from the bright colors in the artwork. If you're going to use three patterns, why not have some fun? Mix it up a bit like I did, and place geometric patterns on an angle. If you're using bright colors, be sure to choose simpler prints like dots, grids and stripes. The colors and the playful placement will liven up any page.

Supplies: Cardstock (Bazzill); patterned paper (Fancy Pants, KI Memories); letter stickers (American Crafts, Doodlebug); brads (Doodlebug); Misc: SP Kimaro font

TOOLS OF THE TRADE

The only tool you technically need for playing with paper is a pair of scissors, but these handy tools will make cropping and piecing a dream.

- **Paper Trimmer.** Trimmers slice and dice paper with precision and ease. I use a guillotine, but use whatever type of trimmer works best for you.
- **Craft Knife and Mat.** A craft knife with a sharp blade is a must-have for cutting out patterns from paper. A self-healing craft mat works well for straight cuts and will protect your work surface. A glass mat will allow you to cut curves and smaller pieces smoothly.
- **Micro-Tip Scissors.** Standard scissors always work in a pinch, but micro-tip scissors, which have short, sharp blades, work best for cutting small or detailed elements like hearts, flowers and fringe.
- **Circle Punches.** The number of shaped punches available is nearly endless, but I find that circle punches are invaluable and versatile. Circles can work with a number of different layout themes, so a few different-sized punches are well worth the investment.

Balancing the Boat

What do I remember about this day? My daughter's complete and utter happiness to be trying something new and loving it. My photos contained a lot of brown and blue ... and banana yellow. Kind of hard to hide that one! So I played up the photos' subtler colors using big blocks of monotone prints. Then I added a bright, multicolored polka dot border to balance the brightness of the banana boat. Remember, the key to using a loud pattern on a page is mixing it with quieter prints.

Supplies: Cardstock (Bazzill); patterned paper (American Crafts, Dude Designs); letter stickers (American Crafts); epoxy stickers (Creative Imaginations); brads (Doodlebug); paper punch (EK Success); Misc: Times New Roman font

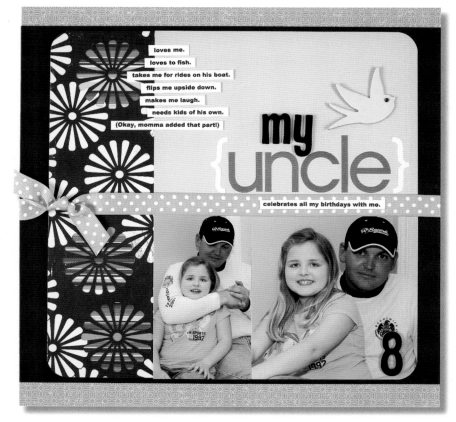

Sneak Peek

To add a feeling of fun to these photos of Michaela with her uncle on her eighth birthday, I wanted to use bright, happy colors. I created an interesting twist on combining patterns by layering a floral die-cut patterned paper over a bold stripe so the stripe peeks through. Mixing three patterns on this page was surprisingly easy: I simply took two of the colors in the stripe (green and black) and chose prints in those colors. Keeping this in mind will ensure your own patterns always work well together.

Supplies: Cardstock (Bazzill); patterned paper (Making Memories, Tinkering Ink); chipboard bird and letters, letter stickers (American Crafts); ribbon (May Arts); Misc: Arial Black font

A Pink Eye

Kelly's daring use of pink print on this travel layout really impressed me. (Pink plus travel—who would've thought?!) With this page, she demonstrates her great eye for design, as well as how your photos can hold the key to placing patterns. Here, you can see how Kelly stacked three patterns to create a "skyline" effect to mimic her bottom photo; she placed her focal photo mostly in the blue "sky" portion. She added a silver print to match the water in her bottom photo, and the pink print brightens her chilly day snapshots. To finish this look, nestle your title along the middle pattern for a balanced design.

Supplies: Cardstock; patterned paper (Heidi Grace, KI Memories); journaling tabs (Heidi Swapp); letter stickers, rub-ons (American Crafts); stamps (Hero Arts); buttons (Autumn Leaves); chipboard heart (Heidi Grace); paper punches (Fiskars); Misc: ink

Artwork by Kelly Purkey

Keeping with the Theme

The mood this Christmas Eve was festive and warm—and a little bit competitive. This turquoise print with little recipes printed inside the dots inspired my design. I mixed it with a pink print that worked with the colors in my photos. To keep with the cooking theme, I printed my journaling on a lined print similar to a recipe card. To achieve this look on your own, balance a themed print with two subtle solid prints to avoid overwhelming your photos.

Supplies: Cardstock (Bazzill); patterned paper (KI Memories, Scenic Route); letter stickers (American Crafts); glitter chipboard letters (Making Memories); brads (Doodlebug); paper punches (EK Success)

A Solid Design

Michaela fell in love with her first kitten, Prissy. Despite her allergies, she lavished Prissy with hugs and attention. I wanted to create a sweet, feminine page for these photos, so I chose three prints from the same pretty collection. When working with busy prints, try choosing a solid background to use as the primary paper in a design, and then adding small pieces of print. For eye-catching detail, you can cut flowers from one of the prints and attach them with adhesive foam squares. Layer silk and paper flowers with a decorative brad for extra dimension.

Supplies: Cardstock, silk flower (Bazzill); patterned paper (BasicGrey); letter stickers (BasicGrey, Doodlebug, Making Memories); epoxy brads and flowers (Making Memories); Misc: Times New Roman font, buttons

A Closer Look

With an obvious watermelon theme, you would think these photos would be easy to scrapbook. Not so much. Sometimes matching paper colors exactly to your photos causes them to get lost. After trying red and green again and again, I placed the photos on this aqua lined paper, which really made them pop. Subtle prints like this one works well as a background. It may not seem that the black-and-red print "goes" with the page, but look closely: The stars are anchored on an aqua grid, which ties the prints together. And the third pattern—a blue polka dot—brings out some of the blue that gets lost in the photos otherwise.

Supplies: Cardstock (Bazzill); patterned paper (KI Memories, Making Memories, Scenic Route); letter stickers, pearl accents (K&Co.); chipboard letters (American Crafts); Misc: 2Peas Composition font

Play with it!

Make an Easy Wave

Materials: Paper, pencil and scissors; optional: flexible ruler

Draw or trace a wave shape on the back side of your patterned paper. (A flexible ruler can be used for precision, but I like the ease and speed of doing it by hand.) Cut along the line.

Flip the small piece you just cut off so the wave is at the top. Place that piece 1-2"(3cm-5cm) below the wave at the top of the larger piece.

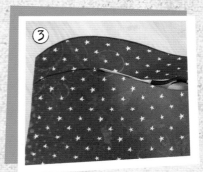

Trace that wave, and then cut along the line.

LUCKY

12 & 23
17 6
15 9
3 1

START WITH ★ IN C...
FIVE NUMBERS ACROSS ANY LINE WI...
VERTICALLY OR DIAGON...
12 DIFFERE...

the BINKY story

Breaking Zach of his binky was not very hard, he only had one he would use
when it got to small for him, I clipped the end off so that it would not work.
I offered him a number of new larger ones, but he would have non of them, he
only wanted his yellow binky, so after about two days of an upset little boy,
we no longer had to use binkys!

It's in the Details

Christine's layout is filled with details that count, but it all begins with this old-fashioned, red patterned background that says "love" to me. She used two other patterns for her embellishments—the leaves are handcut from one, and the chipboard frame is dressed with another. When using a background print to make a statement, include other prints in small amounts to add richness and depth to your design without overwhelming it.

Supplies: Patterned paper (Collage Press, Scenic Route); bingo card, chipboard frame (Jenni Bowlin); letter stickers (Heidi Swapp, Making Memories); label sticker (Li'l Davis); chipboard swirl (Making Memories); brad (K&Co.); crocheted flower (Imaginisce); Misc: Optima Regular font, book page, ink

Artwork by Christine Drumheller

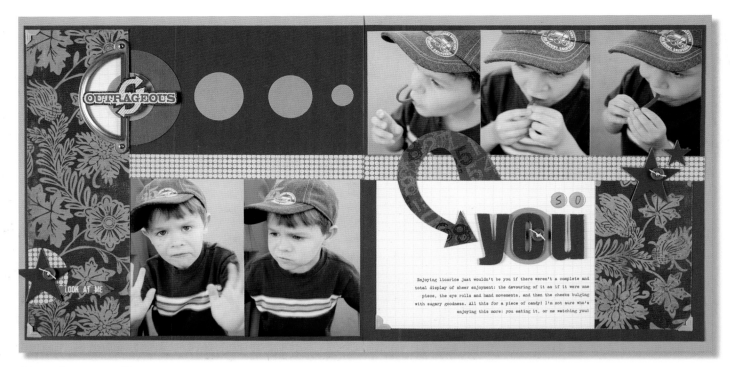

Anchors Away

Jimmy was in his own world with his favorite candy when his mom, Jennifer, snapped these shots. To show off the close-ups, Jennifer chose three prints to anchor various elements on the page. A bold print in navy provides a solid border on each side of the spread. On the left, it holds her creative subtitle, while the block on the right supports the photos. The grid print provides a subtle backdrop for her title and journaling, a technique that will never fail you in achieving good design. The third print, a dotted strip, touches and anchors all the elements and moves your eye across the layout.

Supplies: Cardstock (Bazzill, Prism); patterned paper (Dèjá Views, My Mind's Eye, Scenic Route); letter stickers (Creative Imaginations); chipboard letters (Scenic Route); metal bookplate (BasicGrey); die-cut shapes (Dèjá Views); chipboard stars (Heidi Swapp); buttons (Autumn Leaves); floss (Karen Foster); photo corners (Canson); brads (Making Memories); Misc: Arial font

Artwork by Jennifer Gallacher

Quart, Pint, Ounce

Food is my husband's "thing," and chocolate tops the list. I loved how the "cool" chipboard embellishment fit inside the round bookplate, but I hesitated to use girlie ribbon on a layout about my husband. What to do? Paper to the rescue! I substituted patterned paper for the ribbon holding the bookplate in place. I mixed that bold stripe with two coodinating patterns. In similar colors, the patterns work well together. I also employed the "quart, pint, ounce" principle—using three different amounts of patterns. Use it on your own layouts to keep all the patterns in check.

Supplies: Brads, cardstock (Bazzill); patterned paper (KI Memories); letter stickers (Me & My Big Ideas); brads (Making Memories); chipboard accent (Urban Lily); Misc: 2Peas Evergreen font, ribbon slide

Christmas with a Twist

Christmas layouts in traditional red and green can still hold a bit of the unexpected, as Nicole's layout shows. Her main prints—a simple solid with a pale blue twist and an "almost solid" green dot—are basic rather than Christmas-themed. She keeps the busy holiday tree print to a minimum by cutting out just a few trees and using adhesive foam to layer them on the page. Using bold blocks of one print to sandwich a photo collage nicely frames the page.

Supplies: Cardstock (Bazzill); transparency (Hambly); die-cut cardstock (KI Memories); chipboard shapes, patterned paper (Scenic Route); chipboard letters (BasicGrey); border sticker, letter stickers, tag (Creative Imaginations); Misc: paint

Artwork by Nicole Samuels

3-way Three patterns, three ways

On these pages, three different artists use the same three patterns (above) on a layout. These layouts show that you can mix three patterns effectively in a variety of ways.

Bold but Balanced

Michaela could barely stand up as the boat was moving through the waves, but it didn't stop her from keeping up with the older kids. I wanted bright, colorful papers to convey a sense of fun and excitement to match my photos. So I chose to use the three bold prints each in a simple strip on the page. The small amounts make sure one pattern doesn't overpower the layout. To finish, I used circles and a frame for the focal photo to create a visual triangle.

Supplies: Cardstock (Bazzill); button, patterned paper (KI Memories); chipboard letters (American Crafts); rub-ons (Scenic Route, Urban Lily); photo turn (7gypsies); brads (Making Memories)

July, 2001

ride

PERFECT moments

At 15 months, you are amazed by the movement of the boat, the wind thru your hair, the sound of the water hitting the side, and the other boats passing by. But mostly, you want to hang with the big kids.

Sunny (Almost) Solid

Bright prints can communicate happiness, so the orange paper was the perfect background for Greta's sweet page. While the pattern is bold, the monotone orange print makes it suitable to use as a "solid" background. To be on the safe side, Greta used the other patterns just as an accent border and frame. Take this tip from Greta: Use black-and-white photos to ensure they shine against busy prints, and keep details (like these hearts) bold so they don't get lost on the page.

Supplies: Cardstock (Bazzill); patterned paper (KI Memories); chipboard hearts (Scenic Route); die-cuts, rub-ons (Dèjá Views); buttons (Creative Imaginations); Misc: Batik Regular font

Artwork by Greta Hammond

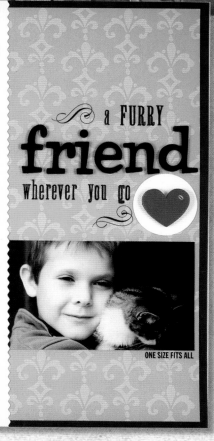

a FURRY
friend
wherever you go

BEYOND MEASURE
Love

1234567890

You are such an animal lover. No matter where we go, you have the uncanny ability to find a furry friend. We stopped at Dr. Sellon's to feed the farm cats and you couldn't resist picking one up. I think the look on your face says it all. I love this about you. A furry friend wherever you go.

ONE SIZE FITS ALL

Heather brought over Wyatt's Buzz Lightyear Bubble Blower, and you two could not wait to try it out. There's something magical about bubbles in the air that makes you chase and pop them for as long as you can catch them. We thoroughly enjoyed watching you two play!

playtime

1 5

Small, Smaller, Smallest

These bright, sunny colors make a great complement to the photos of Jennifer's son, happily enthralled with a bubble machine. Jennifer applied the "quart, pint, ounce" principle to her layout, which has a similar look to Greta's. Rather than use the entire orange print as a background, Jennifer uses it as an accent and fills in the rest of the space with solid orange cardstock. The red circle print anchors the smaller photo contained in a bookplate, and the stripe—the smallest piece—draws the eye to the column of photos.

Supplies: Cardstock (Bazzill, Prism, Provo Craft); patterned paper (KI Memories); decorative tape, epoxy accents, snaps (Making Memories); chipboard letters, photo corners (Heidi Swapp); floss (Karen Foster); tab (SEI); Misc: SP You've Got Mail font

Artwork by Jennifer Gallacher

Evan, 11
Olivia, 11
Austin, 10
Michaela, 6
Marissa, 5

simple things

The five of you are very different.
Each is unique.
But, together, you are family, and
a trip to the pumpkin patch with family
is so much more fun than going alone.

Family

Bits and Pieces

Adding strips or scraps of patterned paper

Too pretty—and too useful!—to throw away, patterned paper scraps make for terrific layout designs. New scrapbookers often say they have a hard time letting go and cutting their full-size papers into smaller pieces. I say go for it! When you know you are going to save the leftovers for another page, you won't feel any guilt for using just a piece. And I'll admit, the thrifty side of me gets a thrill every time I dig into my scrap pile.

What is a scrap? It's anything less than a full sheet, which includes large strips, blocks of print, leftover punches, etc. Even if you're new to scrapping, you probably already have a collection! Once you start using them, you'll find that smaller pieces of patterned paper are much less overwhelming to use. And no matter what patterns you choose, for a no-fail start, begin with a cardstock base and build your design over that. Once you begin mixing them together, I guarantee you'll be addicted to the ease of using bits and pieces!

Color Cues

We all were ready to stretch our legs after the drive to Tennessee, and there were lots of interesting shops to explore while we did. To design a page around the photos, first I identified the colors in them and pulled random scraps from my pile in those colors. On the page, I used the scraps to create a simple photo frame. I placed the larger block of blue on the khaki background, then layered smaller pieces in green and lime. Simple! Complete your own page with a title in colors that contrast with those in the frame (like my orange and brown title) to make the words stand out.

Supplies: Cardstock (Bazzill); patterned paper (BasicGrey, Scenic Route, Me & My Big Ideas); chipboard letters (Heidi Swapp); letter stickers (BasicGrey); brad, metal accent (K&Co.); photo turns (7gypsies); glitter brads (KI Memories); Misc: Times New Roman font

STICK WITH IT

Adhesive is a must-have for working with paper. But choosing the right one can be overwhelming. Stick (pun intended) to these types and you'll always have exactly what you need on hand.

- **Tape Runners.** With their thin widths and variable sizes, tape runners work well for attaching large pieces of paper, strips and even photos. And because they're dry, these adhesives won't bleed through your paper.
- **Glue Stick.** A stick with a wide applicator is the best for attaching paper to chipboard. Adhesives like these can go right to the edge of your chipboard to prevent your paper from rolling up at the edges.
- **Adhesive Dots.** I can't live without my dots! When you want easy, permanent and precise application, adhesive dots will be your best friends. Available in a wide variety of widths and sizes, dots are great for attaching small paper pieces, as well as buttons, chipboard, ribbon, rickrack and other dimensional embellishments.
- **Adhesive Foam.** For paper that really pops, stick with foam! Whether circular or square in shape, adhesive foam gives dimension to all kinds of hand-cut paper details.

Star of the Page

I want my daughter to know she's a star in my book, regardless of how many points she might get in a game, so I played up the star theme fully on this page. To add pizzazz to these black-and-white photos, I chose pieces of several coordinating patterns and cut them into 4" (10cm) panels. I placed them in a row to create one large rectangle, ending with an orange print. For balance, I used additional scraps of orange paper to create a large arrow on the opposite end of the spread. You can use scraps like I did to create custom emebellishments as well.

Supplies: Cardstock (Bazzill); patterned paper (KI Memories); letter stickers (Doodlebug, Me & My Big Ideas); chipboard stars, clear accents (Heidi Swapp); buttons (SEI); brads (Making Memories, SEI); paper punches (EK Success); Misc: Arial Black font

Center Stage

Michaela treats this kitten like her baby, and he's a good sport about it. I added warmth and personality to my simple layout design with these leftover scraps of patterned paper. To create an eclectic page like this, choose a neutral background to allow the photos, framed by the patterns, to take center stage. Add detail to some of the edges with decorative scissors. Minimal embellishments finish this fun page.

Supplies: Cardstock (Prism); patterned paper (KI Memories, Li'l Davis, Scenic Route); letter stickers (Mustard Moon); Misc: AL Handcrafted font

New Paper Column

My youngest has a candy-coated exterior to hide her mischievous inner self, as seen in these Easter photos. To play on the Easter theme, I chose typical spring patterns, but I included black to add some spunk. To re-create this easy look, pick a few colors (like pink, green and blue) and gather together four long strips of patterned paper in those hues.

Place three strips in columns next to your photos. Cut the fourth strip in half lengthwise and place those strips at the top and bottom to frame your block. Consider choosing one pattern with details you can "pop."

Supplies: Cardstock (Bazzill); letter stickers, patterned paper (Scenic Route); rhinestones (K&Co.); rub-ons (American Crafts); flowers, metal letter (Queen & Co.); brads (Doodlebug, KI Memories); Misc: AL Capone font

Play with it!
Cut and Pop Pattern Details

Materials: Patterned paper, craft knife, craft mat, small embellishments (like buttons and brads), adhesive and adhesive foam

① Place your paper on the craft mat. Using a craft knife, cut out a few of the details in the patterned paper design.

② Attach small embellishments like brads and buttons to your cut-out images.

③ Add adhesive foam to your cut-outs. Then reattach them in their original spaces in the pattern. For added dimension, rotate them slighly so they don't line up exactly with the edges of their spaces.

Easy Peasy

So we were a day late. My husband made fun of us, but we went right ahead coloring our eggs anyway. I picked out this solid purple to make my bright photos pop. Then (the best part!) I chose bright patterned paper scraps in shades similar to the photos and placed them to make a super easy border along the bottom of the page. I also used the green pattern to make "egg" embellishments. Green and shades of blue work well with purple, and the small-scale patterns don't compete with the photos.

Supplies: Cardstock (WorldWin); patterned paper (Fancy Pants, KI Memories, Li'l Davis); chipboard letters, brads (Making Memories); letter stickers (Arctic Frog); rhinestones (Heidi Swapp); rub-ons (KI Memories); buttons (SEI); felt flowers (American Crafts); flowers (Bazzill, Prima); Misc: 2Peas Evergreen font

Sew Smart

Sadie might not have understood the Easter Bunny concept, but she looks adorable in her pink bunny ears. Mary's pink and green patterns fit perfectly on this baby bunny page, but the perfection nearly didn't happen. Mary found the green print in too-small sections rather than in one large sheet. Rather than give up, she ingeniously stitched the three pieces together to create a full "sheet." It's a great idea for saving paper as well as adding sweet texture just right for a page like this. Mary also used a scrap of pink to cover her chipboard title letters.

Supplies: Cardstock (Bazzill); patterned paper, ribbon (Making Memories); paper trim (Doodlebug); photo corner (Heidi Swapp); buttons, chipboard letters, rub-ons (American Crafts); rhinestone (Darice); Misc: AL Uncle Charles and Wendy's Hand Medium fonts

Artwork by Mary MacAskill

A Little Goes a Long Way

Irma's use of simple design amazes me. The background is rough, as most boys prefer, but the graphic design and photos of her son make such an impact. Her design shows how very little can go a long way. Just a few colorful strips, slightly woven, add that spark to the layout and frame the photos perfectly.

Supplies: Cardstock (Bazzill); patterned paper (KI Memories, Scenic Route); chipboard letters (Heidi Swapp); brads (Making Memories); Misc: AL Remington font

Artwork by Irma Gabbard

Punch It Up

Nicole wanted to use a long strip of floral paper to create a colorful border for her photo, but her scraps were in too many too-small pieces. Rather than give up on the floral, she employed square punches to make her odd-shaped scraps a uniform size. The result is a lively, graphic border that's more interesting than a long, plain strip. It's a good reminder to us all: Making do can turn out better than doing we intended.

Supplies: Cardstock (Bazzill); patterned paper (American Crafts, Scenic Route); chipboard accents (Creative Imaginations, Making Memories); rub-ons, tag (Creative Imaginations); Misc: ribbon

Artwork by Nicole Samuels

{priceless}

chit chat

grin

It's no wonder that the first telephone number you learned by heart was your Granna's. You love calling her up and chatting about anything and everything. Most times you manage to slip in a request to sleep over at her house. You can't help it. She's one of your favorite people. Not that she spoils you or anything. Yeah, right! Summer, 2006

Seamless Transition

This photo really shows off Michaela's girly side, so I mixed colorful, feminine patterns with ribbon and rickrack on this page. Whether you use one photo or more, this design allows room for lots of journaling and a creative title treatment. I took the pink and orange color cues from the photo and placed the pattern just above to provide a seamless transition from picture to paper. Top your own layout with a black-and-white pattern; it's sure to match and guarantees that it won't overpower the photo.

Supplies: Cardstock (Bazzill); patterned paper (A2Z, Autumn Leaves); chipboard and script letters (Heidi Swapp); rickrack (Wrights); bookplate (BasicGrey); transparency (Hambly); rhinestone brads (Target); ribbon (May Arts); brads (Making Memories); rub-on (Creative Imaginations); Misc: 2Peas High Tide font

Framed

As memory keepers, we are often behind the camera instead of in front of it. I'm glad I was able to take this photo for my sister and her boys, and I wanted to create a beautiful page with it. To do so, I combined a leftover block of pastel floral with strips of a black-and-cream print. The florals keep it fancy, while the layers make it fun. On your own page, incorporate more of one print in your embellishments to tie it all together.

Supplies: Cardstock (Bazzill); patterned paper (A2Z, Scenic Route); letter stickers (Doodlebug); brads (Doodlebug, Making Memories); flowers (Prima); bingo card (Jenni Bowlin); button (Autumn Leaves); Misc: Times New Roman font

Play with it!
Craft a Fancy Photo Mat

Materials: 2 patterned papers, paper trimmer, adhesive, paper piercer and 4 buttons

Cut a piece of patterned paper that is 1½" (4cm) wider and taller than your photo. Place it

Cut four strips of the second pattern that are ¼" (6mm) thick and as long as your layout.

Place the strips around the photo mat. The strips should stretch from one edge of the background paper to the opposite edge. The strips will cross at the corners. Add buttons at the four spots where the strips overlap.

Au Naturel

My husband doesn't allow me to take many photos of him, but he was having too much fun camping to worry about me and my camera. For unfussy, outdoor shots like these, choose patterns that jazz up the page, like these polka dots do. You don't need a lot—just a couple scrap pieces to liven things up. Complement nature-themed photos with coordinating prints containing twigs, leaves or trees.

Supplies: Cardstock (Bazzill); patterned paper (Fancy Pants, KI Memories, Scenic Route); chipboard letters (Heidi Swapp); rub-on (Scenic Route); chipboard accent (K&Co.); brads (Making Memories); Misc: Typist font

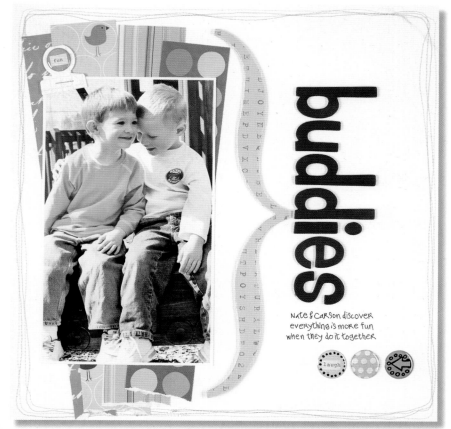

Welcome Mat

Who says photo mats have to be perfect rectangles? Use strips of leftover patterns to create an interesting mat that will be a welcome addition to any design. Christine tore the ends of four strips for added texture and covered a chipboard embellishment with a fifth print. This quick-to-create look translates to lots of styles: For a playful feel, choose funky prints in bright colors, or for a vintage look, choose soft, shabby florals in light pastels.

Supplies: Cardstock (Bazzill); patterned paper (KI Memories, Scenic Route); epoxy stickers (KI Memories); chipboard letters and bracket (Fancy Pants); tab punch (McGill); Misc: paint, thread

Artwork by Christine Drumheller

The Bold and the Beautiful

It was our first time to visit the pumpkin patch with my sister and her children, and we were all thrilled about it. When looking through my scraps, I chose several large pieces that convey that warm feeling of fall with soft colors and a hint of pumpkin. To add some punch, I created a title in bright colors and beautiful prints. The orange in the title overlaps all the patterns, tying them together. But limiting the color to just one area keeps it from overwhelming the page. Create a similar title by following the steps below.

Supplies: Cardstock (Prism); patterned paper (7gypsies, October Afternoon, Scenic Route); letter stickers (BasicGrey); flowers (Prima); buttons (Autumn Leaves); rub-ons (Scenic Route); paper punch (EK Success); Misc: Typical Writer font

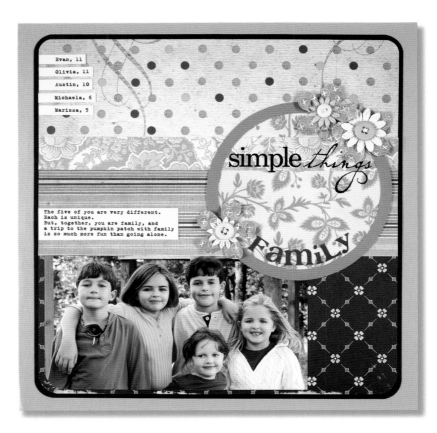

Play with it!
Create a Title in the Round

Materials: patterned paper, cardstock, ruler, circle cutter, adhesive, scissors or paper trimmer, rub-ons and letter stickers

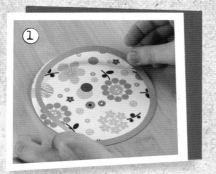

① Cut a circle of patterned paper about 5¼" (13cm) in diameter. Cut a cardstock ring about 5¼" (13cm) in diameter and ⅜" (10mm) thick. Attach the cardstock ring over the paper circle, using adhesive at the top and bottom only.

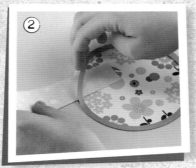

② Cut a strip of patterned paper 1" (3cm) thick and at least 5½" (14cm) wide. Slide the strip between the circle and the ring.

③ Add rub-ons to the strip and additional letters to your circle to complete the title treatment.

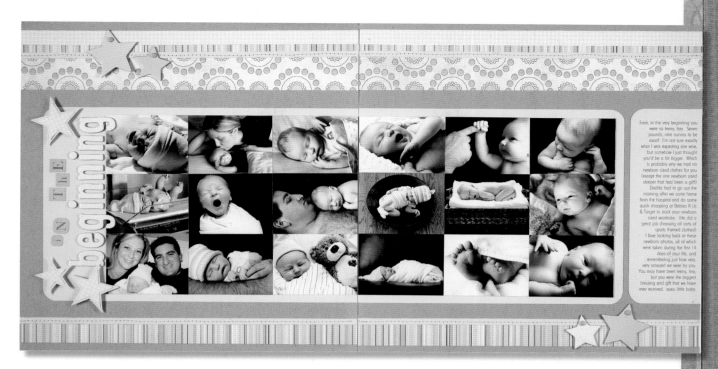

Crossing the Border

Susan captured a lot of sweet images of her newborn baby boy. By printing them small, she was able to include many of her favorites on this layout. Strips of paper create a streamlined border for this graphic collage. You know by now that using strips to create a border is easy. But a border can be interesting, too. Layer your strips to create dimension. Add a strip of cardstock on top, then stitch it to create texture. Placing the strips so they span the entire layout unifies the page. Punch additional scraps into stars, and adhere them with foam for added pop.

Supplies: Cardstock (Bazzill); patterned paper (BasicGrey, Cloud 9, Heidi Grace); chipboard letters and stars (American Crafts); paper punch (Fiskars); Misc: Florida-TS font

Artwork by Susan Weinroth

You've Been Cornered

Michaela and her cousin Marissa are like two peas in a pod. I printed these darling photos in sepia for a timeless appeal and found small pieces of more classic-looking feminine prints left over from another page. For something different, rather than creating a regular square mat, place paper scraps around photos to create an "almost square," leaving the bottom left corners unframed. Then, for polish and balance to the asymmetry, create large photo corners out of additional scraps.

Supplies: Cardstock (Bazzill); patterned paper, photo corners (Daisy D's); chipboard accents (Urban Lily, unknown); flower (Heidi Swapp); brad (Karen Foster); rub-ons (7gypsies); Misc: 2Peas Chestnut font

FAVORITE

hot

SUMMER

Chillin' in the pool has to be your favorite summertime activity. You are lucky to have friends to invite you over, since we don't have a pool. At 12, you aren't yet concerned with tanning. You have more fun diving for rings, splashing anyone who gets close, and jumping off the diving board. Olivia, July, 2007

#1 Idea

Spending time in the pool is one cure for our Mississippi heat. Using your scraps to create large numbers, alphas or shapes is one cure for plain pages. Incorporate patterned paper into your title design by handcutting an extra-large number like my big "1" here. Add additional detail with rub-ons, brads and ink.

Supplies: Cardstock (Bazzill); patterned paper (Autumn Leaves, Fancy Pants, Fontwerks, Me & My Big Ideas); letter stickers (Chatterbox); glitter chipboard (Making Memories); clear accent (Heidi Swapp); rub-ons (BasicGrey, Dèjá Views); pearl stickers (K&Co.); buttons (Autumn Leaves); rhinestones (Me & My Big Ideas); brad (Making Memories); Misc: Times New Roman font

Kick It up a Notch

In these photos, Michaela is talking nonsense to a little bird and loving it, so I felt that simple strips of paper were just a bit boring for this silly page. You can add extra detail to your own scraps by cutting a large decorative edge along one side. Scallops, waves and zigzags can be used with many themes. Then try this technique: Use a die-cut to trace a shape (like this butterfly) on a larger scrap. Cut out the shape just a bit bigger than the outline and layer it under the die-cut with adhesive foam for dimension.

Supplies: Cardstock (Bazzill); die-cut butterfly, patterned paper (K&Co.); rub-ons (BasicGrey, Urban Lily); chipboard accents, rhinestones (Me & My Big Ideas); brads (Doodlebug); scallop trim (Creative Imaginations); Misc: AL Handcrafted font

Piece of Cake

Paper piecing is such a versatile technique, as Kelly shows us here, and it's easier than it looks! You can create anything your imagination will allow. Kelly's buildings created from bits and pieces of patterned paper show her excitement about Chicago. No stencil necessary! Just take a look at your photo, and snip and clip until you've assembled your little city of paper. Add photos, journaling and a title to finish.

Supplies: Cardstock (Bazzill); patterned paper (American Crafts, Heidi Grace, KI Memories); brads, button (American Crafts); stickers (American Crafts, Martha Stewart); paper punch, decorative scissors (Fiskars)

Artwork by Kelly Purkey

Woven Together

Sweet photos on the beach? Ha! My sister related stories of great agony and sweat in her quest for these photos. To highlight her results, I chose scraps of pastel blues and greens (to match the photos), along with orange and brown (for contrast), and created a woven accent block with lots of playfulness and energy. Woven blocks of scrap strips can be used as photo mats, backgrounds or accents to your photos.

Supplies: Cardstock (Bazzill); patterned paper (KI Memories, Prima); chipboard letters (Chatterbox); rub-on (Dèjá Views); button (Autumn Leaves); bookplate (Heidi Swapp); transparency (Creative Imaginations); brads (Making Memories); stickers (Collage Press); Misc: AL Capone font (Photos by Cindy Howell)

TWO Boys

The beach is a favorite place for both of you - as long as you don't have to sit still! This was my reminder of what 'boy' meant - running, jumping, rolling, pushing, being goofy, and for a few very brief moments, smiling those angelic smiles for a hot, sweaty, determined momma with a camera.   July, 2007

Play with it!
Weave a Paper Accent

Materials: Patterned paper, scissors or paper trimmer and adhesive

① Cut eight 1" (3cm) strips of patterned paper.

② Arrange four strips vertically, attaching just the top and bottom of each strip to the page. Arrange the other four strips horizontally over the vertical ones. Attach just one end of each of these strips.

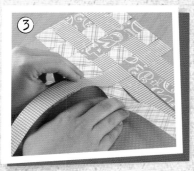

③ One at a time, weave a horizontal strip over and under a vertical strip. Attach the end of each strip to the background.

You really wanted to play outside, despite the fact that we only have dirt right now.

I suppose that it doesn't take much for a boy to go for it and have fun!

{GO!}

venezuela seoul burundi pacific ocean norway ghana vietnam
america guyana cape verde new york cit iti stria nicaragua
africa armenia pacific ocean united states pakista kong albania gabon
and angola united kingdom poland guyana czech republi paraguay belgium yemen
cuba nepal poland atlantic ocean southern ocean canada virgin islands ukraine
guinea nauru algeria philippines

Have Paper, Will Travel

Jennifer's son wasn't going to let a little thing like dirt keep him from having a good time! Jennifer pulled out a scrap of travel paper and used it to tell her story of Jimmy and his outdoor adventure. (How many of us have tried to dig a hole to China?) Sometimes, theme paper can be too much for a page, so using a scrap of it is the perfect solution. Mix the theme paper with a few other strips, and your design is good to go!

Supplies: Cardstock (Bazzill, Prism, Provo Craft); patterned paper (Chatterbox, Dèjá Views, KI Memories); chipboard letters (Scenic Route); rub-ons (Dèjá Views); brackets (American Crafts); labels (Martha Stewart); clips (K&Co.); Misc: Batik Regular, Century Gothic font, circle punch, decorative scissors, ink

Artwork by Jennifer Gallacher

3-way One sketch, three ways

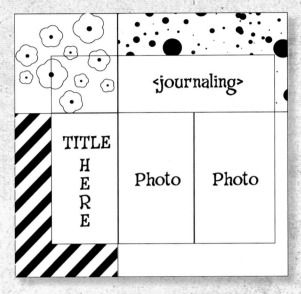

Here, three different artists use the same sketch (above) as the base for a layout. These layouts illustrate how one sketch doesn't just equal one way to use paper pieces successfully on a page.

To a T

Soft blue and yellow prints lend a sweet, serene feel to this page about Susan and her precious little one. On this layout, Susan followed the sketch to a T, turning paper scraps into patterned blocks that became the page's background. Susan added a textured touch with stitching that holds the piece together. Using a sketch and combining patterns from the same manufacturer makes for a no-fail design.

Supplies: Cardstock (Bazzill); chipboard accent, patterned paper (Heidi Grace); chipboard letters (American Crafts); paper punches (Fiskars); Misc: Qurillian font

Artwork by Susan Weinroth

Little Baby. That has been your official nickname since around Day 4, as decided by me, your Momma! I know it's not hugely original, but I still love it, and it was something that just stuck. And even now that you have gotten a bit bigger, you are still my little baby... And always will be!

Flip It, Flip It Good

I wanted to make a funny layout lamenting our lack of snowfall here in Mississippi, so I chose an icy blue plaid and a more playful black print to complement my photo and journaling. Unlike Susan, I flipped the sketch on its side and didn't quite follow the plan.

I placed large blocks of pattern in two opposite corners and left navy cardstock to fill in the rest. I did include some pattern in a third space by using a die-cut machine to create paper snowflakes from various blue scraps. The same technique can work on many themed pages with shapes like spring flowers, Valentine hearts or funky circles.

Supplies: Cardstock (Bazzill); patterned paper (BasicGrey, KI Memories, Scenic Route); letter stickers (American Crafts, Making Memories, Me & My Big Ideas); rub-ons (BasicGrey); rhinestone brads (Making Memories); die-cut snowflakes (Provo Craft); pearls (K&Co.); photo corner (Heidi Swapp); Misc: 2Peas Flea Market font, buttons, sequins

You must be *LOST*

You must be. This is
● Mississippi.
As much as we love snow, and as much as we wish for
● snow.
it rarely snows here. So you see, a
● snowman
in our yard isn't a common sight. You must be
● lost.
Don't get me wrong. You are very welcome here, and you do look rather dashing in your ribbon scarves. I only worry that our
● warm
temperatures will not be quite the thing for you.

February 12th, 2006

Perfect Couple

On her layout, Jenn also flipped the sketch and, in addition, moved the space for journaling down in favor of two unadorned blocks of print. To complement her beautiful photo from her travels through Vancouver, Jenn chose pastel patterns that enhanced the spring theme. Just a couple of small scraps along with a background print make this page "spring" to life. The simple mix of a floral pattern, a striped paper in like colors, and a polka-dotted background add interest to her single-photo layout without overpowering the focal point.

Supplies: Cardstock (Bazzill); buttons, felt flowers, patterned paper (Making Memories); letter stickers (Collage Press); chipboard letters (Li'l Davis); paper trims (Doodlebug)

Artwork by Jenn Olson

We only saw this park from the horse taxi – but it was so lovely, so symbolic of spring. It was hard to tear my eyes from it.

spring IN FULL BLOOM

VANCOUVER, B.C.

MARCH 07

A cool Fender Guitar
a funky skull strap
A touching gift from Warren
A new interest sparked

Cam...August 2007

guitar

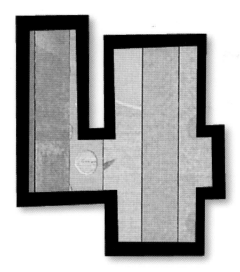

Divine Details

Creating accents with patterned paper

For as long as I can remember, I've helped my mother put up her Christmas tree by shaping the artificial branches, wrapping the tree with hundreds of tiny lights and unpacking boxes of ornaments. Then, she'd take over the decorating. Oh, she would let me assist, but I could tell that she loved adding all the beautiful details herself. In the same way, for many of us, adding details to our scrapbook pages is the best part!

When it comes time to decorating your pages, it's time to let loose. Major decisions about the layout have already been made. You've chosen the colors and patterns that enhance your photos and help tell your story, and you know where everything will be placed. Now you can relax and play with the details! Patterned paper is so versatile. It can be used for creative titles, unique journaling and one-of-a-kind embellishments, as well as great background designs. Using basic tools and supplies like your scissors, craft knife, punches, ink and adhesives, you can add simple details or more complicated ones. It's all up to you. Either way, it's all in the details.

Trimming the Tree

Greta photographs her Christmas décor and baked treats each year for her scrapbook album. She often uses patterned scraps to create unique embellishments like these holiday trees and holly leaves for her pages. Crafting perfectly shaped Christmas trees is easy: First, draw a tree on solid cardstock and cut it out. Then, attach pieces of patterned paper over the cardstock shape and trim around the edges. Mixing patterns in various Christmas shades and topping them with simple buttons gives a page country charm.

Supplies: Cardstock (Bazzill); chipboard accents, patterned paper, stickers (Scenic Route); brads (American Crafts); die-cut shape (Provo Craft); buttons (Creative Imaginations); Misc: ink

Artwork by Greta Hammond

Merry-Go-Round

This round Smile-O-Meter embellishment was just waiting for a layout. When I caught my daughter laughing at her sister and cousins, I knew I had the right photos for it. To repeat the round shape of the title, I used basic circle punches on colorful scraps for quick, inexpensive embellishments. Matting the colorful circles on a white print makes them stand out instantly.

Supplies: Cardstock (Bazzill); patterned paper (7gypsies, K&Co.); chipboard accents (K&Co.); brads (Karen Foster); paper punch (EK Success); Misc: Bodoni MT Black font

Brody is the baby of the family. By that, I mean he is the youngest of your 5 cousins. You are only 11 weeks older than his brother, Joseph, and some might expect for you two to exclude Brody since he is 2 years younger. But, you don't. Instead, you love to have Brody in the midst of whatever you are doing. He thinks you are a hoot, and he loves playing with you. You think he's silly and outrageous and sweet. Sounds like a friendship made to last.

All Aflutter

Why is it that kids seem to have the most fun when they are doing something Mommy doesn't approve of? To highlight these mischievous photos, I used playful patterns to mat and frame the photos. I also used the patterns to enhance acrylic butterfly embellishments. To re-create this look, trace an acrylic shape on the wrong side of the patterned paper and cut it out. Attach the paper shape to the layout, then layer the acrylic shape over it. Add rhinestones or other tiny embellishments for more texture and dimension.

Supplies: Chipboard accents, letter stickers, patterned paper (K&Co.); rhinestones, transparent butterflies (Heidi Swapp);
Misc: Times New Roman font

Ring Around the Rosie

Olivia loves planting flowers and couldn't wait to get her hands dirty. To balance this block of photos, I created an eye-catching border with a sea of custom-made circles. The circles help avoid flower overpower as well as play up the theme in the green background print. Creating the custom details was simpler than it looks: I applied a bunch of bouncing circle rub-ons, then added patterned paper details inside the rings.

Supplies: Cardstock (Bazzill); patterned paper (KI Memories, One Heart One Mind, Scenic Route, SEI); brads, letter stickers (Making Memories); rub-ons (Luxe); stickers (EK Success); rickrack (Wrights); Misc: 2Peas High Tide and Berlin Sands FB fonts

Play with it!
Embellish Rub-Ons

Materials: Ruler, rub-on circles, patterned paper, scissors and adhesive

Measure the inside dimension of your rub-on circles. The measurement will be the diameter of the paper circles in step 2.

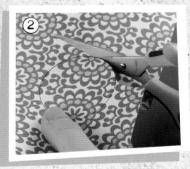

Draw circles on the patterned paper. Cut out the circles.

Rub your image on the layout. Then attach your paper circle to the center of the rub-on circle.

The cape. The wig. They were your choices and you loved your costume. Goodbye, ballerina. Goodbye, Cinderella. Goodbye, Tinkerbelle. What will you come up with next year? Maybe you'll be a pirate with purple hair! Olivia, October, 2007

Frame It Up

I think purple suits her ... or maybe it's the smile. For this layout, I reached for Halloween-themed paper scraps and created a lightly woven photo frame. Don't worry about making your own frame perfect. Trim strips to about the same width and fit them together, with varying lengths and some running off the page. Stickers, die-cut alphabet letters and rings, brads and punched cardstock circles complete this quick, but fun look.

Supplies: Cardstock (Bazzill); patterned paper (KI Memories); die-cut letters (Provo Craft); stickers (Karen Foster); paper punches (EK Success); brads (Doodlebug); Misc: Pea Lacy font

Big and Bold

This page reflects one of my beliefs—that smiles should be shared, and often. I sometimes cut large designs from my patterned papers to use as embellishments, and I thought this easy but bold technique would work well in contrast to this simple photo. Creating this look on your own layouts is easy. Cut a large element from a big pattern, and attach it to your layout opposite a single photo matted on a print with a small-scale design. (You could also use a block of smaller photos.) Keep any other embellishments small.

Supplies: Patterned paper (Creative Imaginations, Daisy D's, Scenic Route); bookplate, letter stickers, rub-on (BasicGrey); flower (K&Co.); brad (Making Memories); Misc: Times New Roman font

Large and in Charge

Caught in the act! But according to Christine, her subject is making some sort of joyful noise all the time. To impart that big, loud, "joyful" feeling, Christine handcut large curls from patterned paper, inked the edges and placed them alongside her photo. She also added journaling along the edges of the swirls. The swirls really command attention, but the photo's enlargement helps it stay center stage. Keep this in mind when choosing patterns for large details: More subtle prints add interest and movement without detracting from the photos.

Supplies: Cardstock (Bazzill); patterned paper (KI Memories, Scenic Route); stamps (Technique Tuesday); die-cut shapes (Scenic Route); letter stickers (Heidi Swapp, Making Memories); ribbon (Heidi Swapp); Misc: 2Peas Favorite Things font, buttons, colored pencils

Artwork by Christine Drumheller

Since she was little, she's always liked making music - especially loud music. At a visit to the children's museum in Nashville, Tennessee, she got the chance to make music on some very big instruments. Michaela, Summer, 2007

being me

mUSiC and mess maker

Contrasting Opinion

Popular opinion may say you must "match" your photos, but with pictures of Michaela that were mostly blues, I decided to use contrasting colors to make the photos pop. For my biggest block of pattern, I chose a red print with zany circle details. To play them up, I added rub-ons around several circles and embellished them with brads. To add pizzazz to the light-colored photos, I chose a multicolored stripe to create a fun photo frame that ties the blue and red on the page together.

Supplies: Cardstock (Bazzill); patterned paper (BasicGrey, Scenic Route); letter stickers (BasicGrey); epoxy stickers (KI Memories); brads (Making Memories); chipboard accents (Urban Lily); rub-ons (American Crafts); Misc: Times New Roman font

Black and White

Can you see the sparkle in my niece's eyes? She's such a girly girl, from her pink suit to her Ariel goggles. I wanted this layout to reflect her colorful, spunky personality so I started with lime green and turquoise papers. But it's the flower details that are the best part, with their funky black-and-white pattern, crumpled texture and shiny centers. Black-and-white papers and accents go well with bright colors, providing a nice contrast and a cool place for the eye to rest.

Supplies: Cardstock (Bazzill); patterned paper (Creative Imaginations, Doodlebug, Me & My Big Ideas); chipboard letters (Heidi Swapp); epoxy accents (KI Memories); rub-ons (American Crafts, Urban Lily); glitter chipboard, rhinestones (Me & My Big Ideas); button (Autumn Leaves); Misc: 2Peas Evergreen font

Play with it!
Make Dimensional Flowers

Materials: Patterned paper die-cut flowers, buttons or epoxy stickers, adhesive and adhesive foam

① Crumple a die-cut flower and then flatten it out a bit.

② Attach a button or epoxy sticker to the center of the flower.

③ Add adhesive foam to the back of the flower, and attach it to your project.

One of our favorite "back to school" traditions – choosing a backpack from the many styles and colors available. Although I always gravitate toward something pink, I let you choose your favorite. You decided on a multi-tone pink butterfly one from Gap. The bold, bright colors and busy pattern matched your personality, too! Michaela, August '06

REMEMBER

i love school

Letter of the Law

The first day of school is always a happy day. Inspired by the large letters on Michaela's backpack, I created a bold title treatment for these first-day photos. Bold prints are suitable for big letters, but pair them with solid or subtle papers for your background to avoid a look that makes you dizzy. Simple embellishments add a nice finishing touch.

Supplies: Cardstock (Bazzill); patterned paper (KI Memories, Me & My Big Ideas, Scenic Route); buttons, die-cut letter template (KI Memories); stickers (Sandylion); rub-ons (Creative Imaginations); paper punch (EK Success); Misc: Typical Writer font

Abstract Art

Amber wanted a flower garden that she could be proud of, so she enlisted her mom's help. I'd say they succeeded! To give a virtual tour of the garden through these photos, Amber created "paths" with strips of patterned paper and felt ribbon. She also used paper to create abstract flower shapes so as not to outshine the real flowers. To create a similar look, cut your own abstract shapes from various patterned papers, lightly sand the edges, and attach them with adhesive foam for dimension.

Supplies: Cardstock (Bazzill); patterned paper (7gypsies, Chatterbox, My Mind's Eye); chipboard letters
(Junkitz); ribbon (Offray); Misc: Angostura and Scriptina fonts, floss

Artwork by Amber Baley

EMBELLISH!

Gorgeous prints and patterns can stand on their own—but why should they have to? When you create your own hand-cut details, add some pizzazz to the pieces with embellishments like these.

- Fabric brads turn standard paper die-cuts into statement pieces.
- Hand-sewn buttons add dimension and sweet detail to paper flowers.
- Glitter glue (like Stickles) lets any element sparkle—and with easy application.
- Heat-embossed stamped images provide smooth texture to a subtle pattern.
- Dimensional gloss medium (like Glossy Accents) gives paper a dimensional sheen.

Clean and Clear

My favorite scrapping colors are blue and green, so it only made sense to use those colors to scrap about some of my favorite things. Patterned papers can pump up your journaling and add visual interest to a page. But paper doesn't have to stand on its own. Attach circles punched from scraps of paper to a printed transparency for a fun, graphic look that adds some texture to the page. Add a variety of embellishments and journaling strips to each circle, keeping the rest of the layout clean.

Supplies: Patterned paper (Autumn Leaves, Fancy Pants, K&Co., KI Memories, Li'l Davis, My Mind's Eye, Prima, Scenic Route); transparency (Hambly); rub-ons (BasicGrey, C-Thru, unknown); chipboard letters and stars (Making Memories); brads (Creative Imaginations, KI Memories); pearls, rhinestones (K&Co.); button (Autumn Leaves); paper punch (EK Success); Misc: 2Peas Evergreen font

On the Fringe

She's always been my sweet girl, and on her twelfth birthday, Olivia wanted her grandmother to bake her cake. I chose papers with her favorite colors of pink, lime and turquoise, and accented the row of cake photos with handmade paper fringe. It's such an easy way to add texture and a little kick! To customize a pre-made chipboard title, use a bit of pattern behind open letters (like this O), and add buttons or brads that repeat the colors in your patterned paper.

Supplies: Cardstock (Bazzill); patterned paper (KI Memories); chipboard title (K&Co.); chipboard letters (American Crafts); rhinestone word (Me & My Big Ideas); buttons (Autumn Leaves, My Mind's Eye); ribbon (May Arts); rub-on (C-Thru)

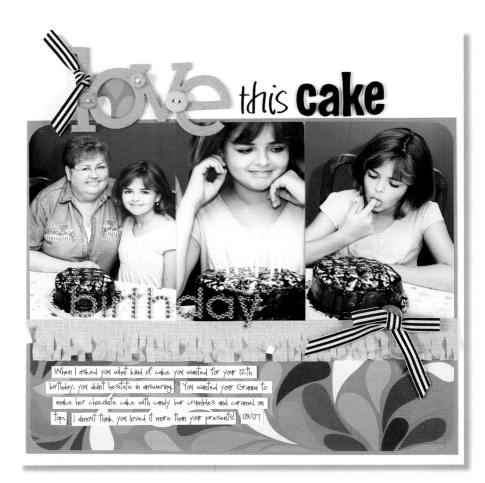

When I asked you what kind of cake you wanted for your 12th birthday, you didn't hesitate in answering. You wanted your Granna to make her chocolate cake with candy bar crumbles and caramel on top. I almost think you loved it more than your presents! 09/07

Play with it!
Cut Paper Fringe

Materials: Patterned paper, micro-tip scissors and adhesive

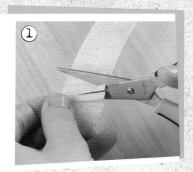

Cut a 1" (3cm) wide strip of patterned paper to your desired length. Using the scissors, make vertical cuts about ¾" (2cm) into the strip and about ¼" (6mm) apart.

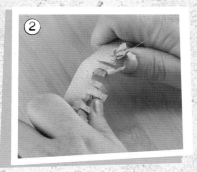

Crumble the fringe gently. Then flatten the fringe a bit.

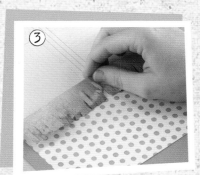

Attach the top, uncut edge of the strip to your project with a line of adhesive.

A hype is what all of you involved in the band and colorguard call it. During band camp in August this is what you guys do to "hype" everyone up for the band season. Or at least that is why I think it's called a hype. Every day there is a different theme and everyone who wants to will dress up according to the theme. It's a whole lot of fun for everyone and it really does make the long rehearsals fun. This day the hype was "Mix-Match". You really went all out with your crazy outfit!

HYPe

say what??

LIVE·LAUGH·LOVE

play·ful (plā´fil) adj. 1.Lightly humorous; joking. 2.Full of high spirits and play; frolicsome.

Mix and Match

Irma's photos of her teenage daughter give me a little glimpse of what I'm in for! Got busy photos? Choose light-colored cardstock to act as your base. It's OK to add some mix-and-match print and color to pages with busy photos. Just be sure to limit them to a few places on the page, like in borders and titles. You can create a fun title treatment like Irma's using your own patterned scraps. Handcut (or die cut) letters in your title out of different patterned papers, and layer "negative" images over other patterns.

Supplies: Cardstock (Bazzill); patterned paper (EK Success, KI Memories, Provo Craft); rub-on (SEI); brad (American Crafts); Misc: 2Peas High Tide font

Artwork by Irma Gobbard

Circle Reincarnation

I love the bright colors in these photos and chose three patterned papers that repeated the red, pink and turquoise in them. On the layout, circles are reincarnated as an interesting scallop border in my brightly hued patterns. To create a similar look, cut several circles in different sizes from various papers. Tuck them under the top and bottom edges of your photos. You can mix circle-shaped rub-ons with the paper circles for an unexpected design twist. Round out your title, journaling and additional accents to complete the look.

Supplies: Cardstock (Bazzill); patterned paper (Autumn Leaves, KI Memories); chipboard letters (American Crafts); brads (Doodlebug); rub-ons (Hambly); paper punches (EK Success); Misc: Times New Roman font

Circular Logic

I'm a firm believer that circle punches are a scrapper's best friend. They are the most versatile of tools, as Cari demonstrates with her stunning layout. The curvy join of the two pieces of cardstock is a neat touch, and she takes it further by adding punched paper circles in various sizes along with buttons and rub-ons. Cari repeats that circle shape in her title to tie in the theme. Although Cari used coordinating patterns, this design can be interpreted using many different prints.

Supplies: Cardstock (Bazzill); chipboard accents, patterned paper, rub-ons (BasicGrey); chipboard letters (Heidi Swapp); letter stickers (Scenic Route); buttons (Autumn Leaves); Misc: Arial font, ink

Artwork by Cari Locken

Stamp Your Art Out

I certainly didn't have a hand in caring for this rosebush. If I had, it wouldn't have lived long! With such bold colors, I wanted to be careful not to compete with the photos. Instead, I chose subtle papers in hues similar to, but subtler than, my roses to use as my background. I added just a little contrast with the stamped embellishments. Yes, you can stamp on patterned paper! Create one-of-a-kind embellishments by combining simple stamps with your patterned paper stash.

Supplies: Cardstock (Bazzill); patterned paper (7gypsies, K&Co.); ribbon (May Arts); stamp (Fontwerks); letter stickers (American Crafts, Creative Imaginations); paper punches (EK Success); clip (7gypsies); Misc: ink

Ruffling Feathers

Michaela always ends up with half of her ice cream on her face. But she does look like an angel eating it. For this sweet summertime page, I chose soft warm colors for the background and matched the colors in Michaela's outfit (pink, orange and green) in the details. Instead of using ribbon or trim, I added a ruffle of golden-colored patterned paper to add playful feminine detail to this layout about my little girl.

Supplies: Cardstock (Bazzill); patterned paper (Autumn Leaves, Making Memories); chipboard letters (American Crafts); letter stickers (BasicGrey, Making Memories); flowers, lace tape (K&Co.); rhinestones (Prima); rub-on (Scenic Route)

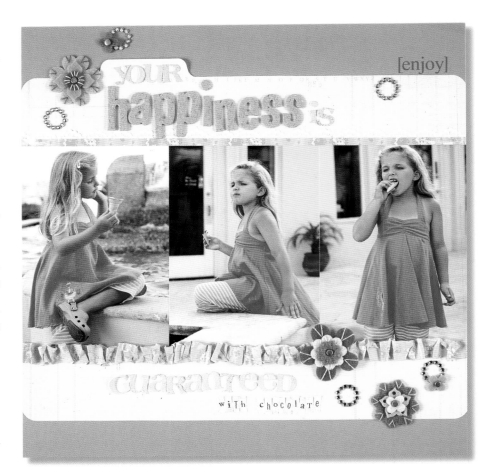

Play with it!
Ruffle Your Trim

Materials: Patterned paper, scissors or paper trimmer and adhesive

Cut two strips of paper about 12" (30cm) long and ¾" (2cm) wide. Attach the two strips at their ends to create one long strip.

Gently crumple the strip. Apply a line of adhesive to your layout where you'd like the trim to be.

Fold under one end of the strip and attach it to one end of the adhesive line. Attach the rest of the strip by scrunching and sticking along the line of adhesive.

It's tradition at your school when getting asked to go
to Homecoming that the boy asks you by bring you
flowers of some kind and asking you at school in front
of your friends. Today it happened to you for the first
time. You were given a bouquet of flowers and a stuffed
animal and he asked you in the lunch area in front of
all your friends. You told me that everyone around you
clapped after you said 'yes'. What an exciting
Homecoming for you!

In Stitches

Irma's daughter looks so pretty with her bouquet of flowers. To play up the occasion's sweet and formal mood, Irma used a large piece of black-and-cream floral pattern and coupled it with more playful, casual elements. She took a different take on using patterned paper details: Rather than using the paper to create small elements, she added details—like glitter glue and stitching—to the paper. Additional red-and-cream patterns add color to the design.

Supplies: Cardstock (Bazzill); patterned paper (7gypsies, Die Cuts With A View, My Mind's Eye, Scenic Route); word strip (Scenic Route); label (K&Co.); buttons (Autumn Leaves); Misc: 2Peas Hot Chocolate font, floss

Artwork by Irma Gabbard

3-way One sketch, three ways

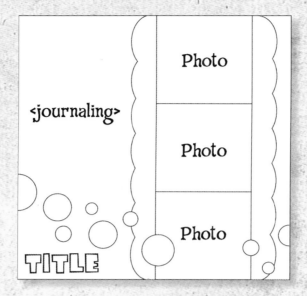

Here, three different artists use the same sketch (above) as the base for a layout. The artists show that you can make a sketch your own using paper details in different ways.

Going in Circles

Like the rest of my nephews, my niece and my daughters, Austin is blessed with big blue eyes. For this layout, I chose a distressed blue pattern to highlight those eyes, and my accents came straight from a coordinating print. After flipping it on its side, I took this simple sketch to the next level with a wave of paper circles that stagger down the page, overlapping the photos. I added dimension to the circles by embellishing them with chipboard stars, rhinestones and brads.

Supplies: Cardstock (Bazzill); patterned paper (Fancy Pants); glitter letters, rhinestones (Me & My Big Ideas); letter stickers (American Crafts, Arctic Frog); brads, chipboard stars (Making Memories); rub-ons (Urban Lily); Misc: Arial Black font

A.Y.

I never heard you complain about wearing braces. You were the first one of the cousins to wear them, but you won't be the last. I hope you save some advice for Olivia and Michaela, because they will need it!

May, 2006

boy with BRACES

make your dreams come true

Musical Highlights

Not a "rebel" like me, Amber used the sketch as is. But her layout is anything but ordinary. She chose patterned papers that repeated the colors in her photos—black, cream and gray with a pop of red—and used those patterns only as accents. Amber kicks her circles up an octave, rumpling and distressing them to create a dimensional, textured scallop border that shows off her photos. She also used patterned paper to dress chipboard brackets that highlight just one photo.

Supplies: Cardstock (Bazzill); patterned paper (BasicGrey); chipboard letters and accents (Bazzill, BasicGrey, KI Memories, Making Memories, Queen & Co.); brads (Queen & Co.); Misc: Will & Grace font, buttons

Artwork by Amber Baley

Shining Examples

Linda created a shabby but chic layout with advice for her daughter by following the layout of the sketch. The soft blue-and-gray pattern really complements the sepia-toned photos. While closely following the sketch as Amber did, Linda broke from the pack with her details, adding glitter to paper stars to really make her page shine. To create the sparkling accents, Linda punched stars and other shapes from different prints, added some adhesive, and generously sprinkled on glitter. A splash of color in the title adds a finishing touch.

Supplies: Cardstock (Prism); patterned paper (Autumn Leaves, BasicGrey, Creative Imaginations); chipboard letters (Making Memories); chipboard stars (BasicGrey); paper punches (EK Success); glitter (Martha Stewart); Misc: Amery font

Artwork by Linda Albrecht

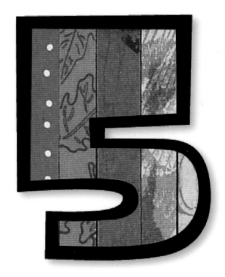

Lots of Layers

Layering different papers on a page

The world around us is full of layers. Thumb through any home decorating magazine to see artful layering of colorful paint, fabrics and trims. Gaze at a famous oil painting, and notice the layers of color applied to the canvas. Reach for your favorite lasagna recipe for yummy layers. Like a piece of gorgeous art or a delicious dinner, layering adds depth and richness to scrapbook pages. I love how patterned paper layers enhance photos and the stories they tell.

With layering papers comes multiple patterns. Unsure how to begin? Take a look back at Chapter 2 for a reminder about successful pattern combinations. Choosing patterns from one manufacturer's collection is a good place to start. For soft drama, choose different patterns in the same color family. For a bold look, choose a big pattern layered with more subtle prints. For texture, distress the edges of your layers. In this chapter, you'll find ideas for layered photo mats and frames, borders and embellishments in addition to background layers. With so many design ideas, by the end of this chapter, you'll be lovin' lots of layers, too.

My sweet baby Zach
so small and new
Love those little back wrinkles
and your dimpled chin too!

Shabby but Chic

Zach's baby face is the first thing you notice here, but it's not long before you begin to notice the beautiful layered details as well. Christine created a soft, shabby frame to highlight the close-up of her little one. To create her framing technique, she started with three patterned paper strips, two of which included a thin strip layered over a thicker strip. She crafted mitered corners and then stitched the edges together. But the layers don't stop there. Patterned paper details, like the tags and the simple diamonds, sit atop the layers of background paper. Journaling strips make up the final layer.

Supplies: Patterned paper (Autumn Leaves, Making Memories); letter stickers (Making Memories); letter stamps (PSX); rhinestones, transparency (My Mind's Eye); paper punch (Emagination Crafts); die-cuts (QuicKutz); Misc: Traveling Typewriter font, ink, photo corners, thread, string

Artwork by Christine Drumheller

WHAT'S THE ALTERNATIVE?

Scrapbook paper is by far the best product for sturdy, safe, acid-free—and gorgeous!—paper crafting. But when you want unique patterned accents, try these alternatives:

- Gift wrap
- Wallpaper scraps
- Maps and atlases
- Fabric

- Office supplies like graph paper and ledger pages
- Paper grocery bags (for Kraft cardstock details)
- Newsprint and old book pages
- Greeting cards

You are always talking. Always! To anyone who will listen. You are friends with everyone you meet. A true

social
BuTterfLy

Layers Come to Life

Have you heard the phrase "she would talk to a wall"? Lisa says it much nicer on this page about her daughter's friendly tendencies. Lisa chose this flocked butterfly print to coordinate with her title, and she added details that pop. To make her butterflies flutter down the page, she simply cut out a few of the butterflies from another piece of the same print and then layered them over their butterfly twins with adhesive foam. Layers of more subtle papers let the butterflies become the life of the page.

Supplies: Cardstock (Die Cuts With A View); patterned paper (Cloud 9); chipboard letters (Heidi Grace); letter stickers (Autumn Leaves); paper punches (Fiskars); Misc: TypeWrong font

Artwork by Lisa Storms

Flower Power

I wanted to tell this darling story about my daughter and her cousin, and chose flowers to convey that sweetness. For your own sweet page, choose distressed, shabby florals and stripes for a feminine, vintage feel. Here I chose a simple, decorative-edge paper to double as a photo mat and journaling block. To re-create a page like mine, use layers to create a "pot of flowers" by stacking circles punched from scraps of paper. Add handcut strips of paper and rub-on "leaves" to complete the arrangement.

Supplies: Patterned paper (K&Co., KI Memories, Li'l Davis, Making Memories, My Mind's Eye, Scenic Route); chipboard accents, paper ribbon, rub-ons, stickers (K&Co.); Misc: 2Peas Fairy Princess font

Play with it!
Create Layered Flowers

Materials: Patterned paper, circle punch or scissors, adhesive, floss, needle and button

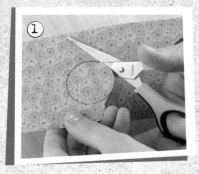

① Punch or cut circles in two sizes from different patterned papers.

② Gently crumple the circles, and then flatten them somewhat. Add adhesive around the edges of the smaller circle (on the back), and then place it on top of the larger one.

③ Stitch a button to the center of each "flower."

Expert Panels

Michaela loves animals, and they love her. I wanted to accent these photos with a layered panel created with strips of various blue and green prints. For a shabby but still streamlined look, I distressed the edges of each strip. As you build your own block of strips, slightly overlap the edges to give your page some added dimension. Layer the patterned panels over cardstock and then over a background pattern for a look with even more depth.

Supplies: Cardstock (Bazzill); patterned paper (7gypsies, Making Memories); chipboard title (K&Co.); brads (Die Cuts With A View); felt flowers (Making Memories); silk flowers (Prima); buttons (Autumn Leaves); Misc: 2Peas Evergreen font

A Soft Touch

To add depth to her layout about her daughter's relationship with her daddy, Nicole simply layered three patterns in similar soft colors behind her photos. Nicole smartly chose the pattern with a corner detail to serve as the background. The plainer green pattern anchors the title treatment as well as the butterfly accent above the photos. The pale ledger pattern provides contrast and an additional photo mat to highlight the picture of daddy and daughter. The soft colors lend a sweet feel to her layout without overwhelming her photos.

Supplies: Cardstock (Bazzill); patterned paper (BasicGrey, Making Memories); buttons, transparent letters (Making Memories); clear butterflies (Heidi Swapp); Misc: Will and Grace font

Artwork by Nicole Samuels

On a Roll

Jenn's layout highlighting her beautiful wedding photos is filled with subtle layers. To create an elegant backdrop for the photos, Jenn layered three monochromatic patterns in classic red. She tore the edges and gently rolled them with her fingertips. The distressed rolls add texture, dimension and some shabby chic romance to the spread. Jenn also chose solid cardstock to mat a few of her photos, using adhesive foam to layer those over unmatted photos.

Supplies: Cardstock, large flower, small brad (Bazzill); patterned paper (My Mind's Eye); brad, die-cut paper, transparent letters (Making Memories); photo turns, stickers (7gypsies); pins, sequins (Paper Relics); large flowers (Prima)

Artwork by Jenn Olson

Got the Blues

Linda has perfected the art of layering. To mat these close-ups of her son, she added layer upon layer of blocks in different patterns, most of which are in the same color family. But take special notice of Linda's use of blue. One of her layers is a blue pattern, that, when set among her other layers, makes them pop. Why? The complementary color tones create an eye-catching contrast. The blue is repeated around the page—in the painted edges and chipboard title—to tie it all together.

Supplies: Patterned paper (Creative Imaginations, Melissa Frances); chipboard letters (Making Memories); stamp (Melissa Frances); brads (Provo Craft); decorative scissors (Fiskars); Misc: Indy 17 font, paint

Artwork by Linda Albrecht

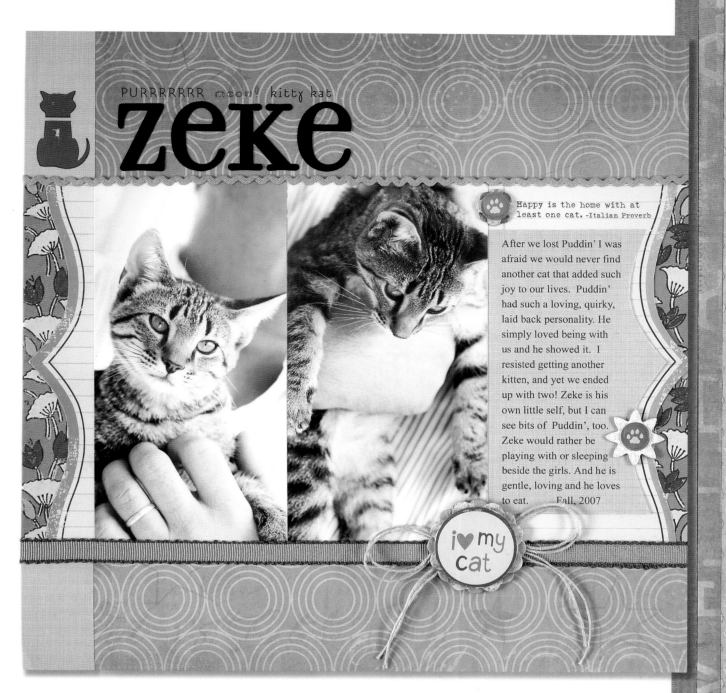

PURRRRRRR meow! kitty kat
zeke

> Happy is the home with at least one cat. -Italian Proverb

After we lost Puddin' I was afraid we would never find another cat that added such joy to our lives. Puddin' had such a loving, quirky, laid back personality. He simply loved being with us and he showed it. I resisted getting another kitten, and yet we ended up with two! Zeke is his own little self, but I can see bits of Puddin', too. Zeke would rather be playing with or sleeping beside the girls. And he is gentle, loving and he loves to eat.   Fall, 2007

i ♥ my cat

Edging out the Competition

These are the first photos I took when we brought our new kitten home. I sandwiched the happy photos on this page with a cheerful floral print. To allow for some breathing room between the photos and the print, I layered a neutral-colored paper with a decorative edge over the floral pattern. The bracket-edge paper also works to frame my journaling and photos, drawing the eye right to them. You can create a bracket-edge journaling block perfectly suited to your page by tracing the decorative paper's edge onto cardstock and cutting a block to size.

Supplies: Patterned paper (7gypsies, Chatterbox, Making Memories, Scenic Route); letter stickers (Making Memories); chipboard and epoxy accents, rub-ons (K&Co.); ribbon, rickrack (BasicGrey); Misc: Times New Roman font

Wave of Inspiration

This is the only time my brother has ever requested that I take a photo of him. (I think the big fish had something to do with it.) On this layout, I enhanced the feeling of my brother's lakeside excitement with wavy lines of paper running down the sides. To enhance your own outdoor photos, use patterns with lots of brown, green and tan like the ones I used here. Papers with a distressed look and copper brads add a rustic touch. After cutting distressed papers, apply ink along the edges to soften them.

Supplies: Letter stickers, patterned paper (BasicGrey); brads (KI Memories); Misc: Times New Roman font, ink

His Catch

You have to know my brother. He grew up with 3 big sisters. Those sisters all love to take photos, and he hates being in front of the camera. So, imagine my surprise when I receive a phone call asking me if I have time to take some photos...of him. I finally managed to drag the story out of him, before racing to the boat dock to take the photos he requested. He loves to fish better than anything. And, catching this whopping 12 lb. 10 oz. bass on Bay Springs Lake was a thrill for him. Being able to take these photos of him with his catch was a thrill for me. Good to know that sisters are good for something! 12/06

Play with it!
Cut a Wavy Border

Materials: Four 2" (5cm) strips of patterned paper, pen or pencil, scissors or craft knife, ink and adhesive

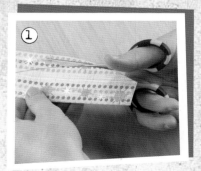

① Draw a wavy line on the back side of your first patterned paper strip, keeping in mind that the wave will be reversed on the front side. Then cut along that line.

② Using the first piece as your guide, draw a wavy line in the opposite direction on the back side of your second patterned strip, and cut along that line. Using this second piece, repeat to create two more pieces.

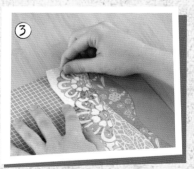

③ Apply ink to the edges of your waves, and attach them (back side down) to your project, overlapping as desired.

Snow Clever

Just looking at Linda's snow photos makes me long for a little of the white stuff. She layered four different patterns to create a cozy winter wonderland that coordinates with the yellow-and-blue photo of her son. The layers I really love are those Linda used to create the title, cleverly layered over two painted tags. The layers of paper and chipboard, along with glitter and sequins, atop the patterned paper background create a dimensional look that makes a big impact.

Supplies: Patterned paper (BasicGrey, Melissa Frances); chipboard accents and tags, stamp (Melissa Frances); chipboard letters (Heidi Swapp); sequins (Westrim); ribbon (May Arts); Misc: Book Antiqua font

Artwork by Linda Albrecht

Formal and Fun

Although these photos were taken at a wedding, the layout is really about the friendship I share with Janet. I wanted to convey a bit of wedding formality, with a lively little twist to match Janet's personality and the playful kissing photo. To accomplish this, I created a photo mat with one formal print layered under a brighter, more playful pattern in blue and green. I also layered a scalloped paper trim, soft ribbons and rickrack to create a dimensional border, and topped it off with buttons to play up the casual feel.

Supplies: Cardstock (Bazzill); patterned paper (K&Co., Paper Studio); letter stickers (BasicGrey, Making Memories); velvet ribbon (Making Memories); flowers (K&Co.); buttons (Autumn Leaves); brads (7gypsies); rickrack (Wrights); Misc: 2Peas Evergreen font

3-way Four papers, three ways

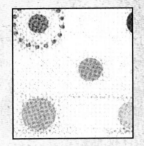   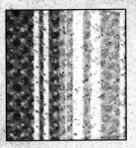

Here, three different artists use the same four papers (above) on a layout. These layouts show you can layer papers in a variety of ways to create different looks and enhance photos.

Torn and Textured

Linda chose to use the polka dot pattern as her background, creating a playful feel for these pet photos. The orange pattern acts as her photo mat, layered over the background, and she layered the floral and the stripe as accent strips. She also demonstrates that patterns in traditional fall colors can be used for other photos and stories.

Supplies: Patterned paper (BasicGrey); buttons (BasicGrey, Prym); letter stickers (Doodlebug, Mustard Moon); rickrack (Wrights); brads (Creative Imaginations); rub-ons (Daisy D's); Misc: Euphorigenic font

Artwork by Linda Albrecht

Part of the family.

We sure do love LuLu, Cole and Becky's little Boston terrier. She is quick and wirey and gets so excited when she comes to visit that she runs Figure 8's from our living room into the dining room. She likes to play fetch with a ball, so we keep one handy for when she is at our house. She is a really fun dog, even though you have to always be on the lookout for her sloppy kisses to your face. LuLu Belle, we love that you are a part of the Family!

AUGUST '07

Solidly Simple

Jennifer's page, featuring little boy photos enhanced by warm paper tones, uses the four patterns as successfully as Linda, but with a more streamlined effect. The almost equal parts of each pattern create balance on the page that's complemented by the symmetry in the design. Jennifer's layers start with solid cardstock tucked behind the patterns. The striped pattern, layered over the pictures' edges, creates a simple photo frame. And the layers in the title treatment tie the look together.

Supplies: Cardstock (Bazzill); patterned paper (BasicGrey): chipboard letters (Li'l Davis, Scenic Route); chipboard stars (Heidi Swapp); brads (Making Memories); Misc; Century Gothic font

Artwork by Jennifer Gallacher

Going to New Heights

In my hurry to catch photos of Marissa roasting marshmallows, I overexposed some, so I converted those to black and white. With the photos saved, I went to work layering the fall-colored papers. Like Jennifer, I applied the patterns in simple layers and used the striped print to create a frame for the photo strip. I used the darkest print to draw attention to my focal photo, creating dimension by layering the paper over a chipboard frame. The most solid print—the orange—does the job of anchoring the other patterns and providing a pleasing place for the journaling.

Supplies: Cardstock (Bazzill); letter stickers, patterned paper (BasicGrey); chipboard frame (Fancy Pants); brads (KI Memories); Misc: High Tower Text font

No doubt about it.

Anyone who meets her will definitely agree.

Chelsea Elizabeth

12 months old

she is

PeRFeCT

Inspiration Station

Designing pages inspired by patterned paper

It has happened to all of us. We gather our special photos, choose our patterned papers and embellishments, and are excited about starting our layout … and then we sit and stare at all of it, wondering where to start. How do you get past that initial freeze?

Look to papers for design inspiration. The very items sitting in front of you can provide just the spark you are looking for. It might be a graphic element or shape that you can repeat in your layout, a lettering or journaling idea or an image that can be copied to create a custom embellishment. Handcutting images directly from a pattern is one of my favorite techniques. It is fast, inexpensive and can give your design instant personality. Even before you sit down to do a layout, patterned paper can inspire. Keep an eye out when you're strolling down the aisle of your favorite scrapbook store—you just might pick up a pattern that will later inspire you to scrapbook certain photos or tell a particular story, like Mary did with her "2007" layout on page 95. Whatever the case, there is no doubt that patterned papers can inspire great pages.

Graphic Design

I chose these coordinating patterns—the concentric shapes, the stripes and the pink flowers—to match my photos, and then I asked myself, "What now?" Instead of cutting details from a design, I let the design dictate my details. The concentric squares inspired me to surround my photos and journaling with a set of nested boxes created by thin strips of white and beige. To break up the severity of the graphic design, I sprinkled more feminine fonts along the top of the page and included floral accents. Try out geometric prints; they can provide tons of inspiration for modern page designs.

Supplies: Brads, cardstock (Bazzill); patterned paper (Chatterbox); letter stickers (BasicGrey); rub-ons (Junkitz); chipboard accents (CherryArte); flowers (Prima); paper punch (EK Success); die-cut lace (K&Co.); Misc: Times New Roman font

Piece Talk

Lisa knows there is nothing sweeter than those first few moments with a new baby in the family. She chose a paper for her layout that included little baby designs doodled all over. Papers in hand, she created her own embellishments based on designs found in the background paper—handcutting a detail to use in her title and also piecing together a peapod out of coordinating papers. Look to your whimsical prints for embellishment ideas that go beyond the basic and will perfectly suit your page.

Supplies: Cardstock (Die Cuts With A View); patterned paper (Heidi Grace); letter stickers (American Crafts); decorative scissors, paper punches (Fiskars); Misc: TypoSlab Light font

Artwork by Lisa Storms

Time to Design

Mary's adorable layout will become a treasure for little Sadie Jane. Mary's inspiration: a patterned paper printed to resemble a page of ads in a vintage newspaper. The newspaper theme gave Mary the idea to document facts about the year Sadie was born, including the major headlines, best-selling books, popular TV shows and prices of groceries. Without the patterned paper, Mary would have missed the chance to record this information. With so many themes, patterned papers can easily inspire layout ideas.

Supplies: Cardstock (Bazzill); patterned paper (Collage Press, Imagination Project, Sandylion); vellum (Paper Co.); chipboard letters, rickrack (American Crafts); flower (Doodlebug); ribbon (Offray); buttons (Autumn Leaves); pins (Heidi Grace); Misc: AL Uncle Charles and Wendy's Hand Medium fonts

Artwork by Mary MacAskill

Cut It Out

These photos of Chelsea demanded a girly, springtime page, and this pastel botanical print inspired handcut embellishments. Swirls, butterflies, flowers—so many different images can be used for custom embellishments. When handcutting elements, trim details with sharp-tipped scissors for a perfect cut and attach them to your page with adhesive foam, overlapping the photos for a little drama.

Supplies: Cardstock (Bazzill); patterned paper (K&Co., Me & My Big Ideas); chipboard and clear letters (Heidi Swapp);
felt accents, photo corners (K&Co.); letter stickers (BasicGrey); Misc: Times New Roman font
(Photos by Donna Garza)

ORGANIZATION STATION

So you've got all that pretty paper—where do you keep it? Keep paper organized with one, or more, of these simple solutions. Be sure to buy containers larger than 12" × 12" (30cm × 30cm) so papers don't get squashed or bent.

- **Hanging Files.** Those made specifically for scrapbook paper (available from companies like Cropper Hopper and Making Memories) allow for a bird's eye view of your collection.
- **Accordion Files.** With divided sections, accordion files are great for organizing small collections of paper, plus those with shoulder straps make your papers portable for crops.
- **Paper Trays.** Clear trays offer a way to see much of your collection at once, and most are stackable, making these a good option for small spaces.
- **Pizza Boxes.** Empty (and clean!) boxes are the perfect size for storing stacks of paper. Label the outside of each box with the contents and stack them as high as the sky!

surf's up dude

Say It Like It Is

Sometimes it's not the look of a pattern that guides your design, but the words that send you on your way. I gathered inspiration for this layout, with photos of a little guy dipping his toes in the sea, after finding a paper with summer words printed in horizontal bands. I cut four strips of that paper and used it to frame my photos. To carry on the design, I added patterned paper in similar colors above and below the gallery of photos. I embellished the page with pieces of die-cut aqua paper. Reminiscent of waves, the pieces enhance the feeling of being by the sea.

Supplies: Cardstock (Bazzill); patterned paper (Autumn Leaves, unknown); die-cut cardstock (KI Memories); acrylic letters (Heidi Swapp); rub-ons (BasicGrey, C-Thru, KI Memories, Scenic Route); flowers (Prima); brads (Doodlebug); Misc: Typical Writer font (Photos by Cindy Howell)

Center Stage

I love these close-ups of my daughter, as they show little glimpses of her personality. As you know, I like to cut elements from my patterned paper. Even with this simple technique, you can still create a coordinated design that really stands out. For this layout, I cut out the leaves from my pattern, but I arranged them on the page in an interesting way. By placing the leaves on white cardstock, they end up looking quite different from their twins in the pattern, delivering a design punch. While attaching the cut-out leaves, I was careful to reposition them in their original "spots" (with the stripes going across the page), making the design look cohesive.

Supplies: Cardstock (Bazzill); patterned paper (Autumn Leaves); chipboard title (K&Co.); rub-ons (BasicGrey, C-Thru); brads, flower, heart (Making Memories); Misc: Times New Roman font

Ahead of the Curve

I could easily be jealous of Irma's garden! Aren't these photos gorgeous? Irma chose a curvy pink-and-green pattern that resembles vines to place behind her title and along the opposite page. Then she used the pattern as inspiration for handcut green vines that accent the page. To enhance the details, Irma added handwritten journaling that follows the curved edges.

Supplies: Cardstock (Bazzill); patterned paper (BasicGrey, Chatterbox); phrase stickers (7gypsies); chipboard letters (Zsiage)

Artwork by Irma Gabbard

Growing Up

My nephew was determined to hide from me as I tried to take these photos on Awards Day. Having two girls, I often struggle for embellishment ideas appropriate for boys, and scrapping these photos was no exception. Fortunately, I found some bold prints with funky circles and flocked vines, which provided the inspiration I needed. I handcut details from the patterns, but instead of stopping at small elements, I cut a whole vine to create a lively border that looks like it's growing up the page. Stuck with how to scrap your photos? Look at your stash of patterns for inspiration to strike.

Supplies: Cardstock (Bazzill); patterned paper (BasicGrey, Chatterbox); phrase stickers (7gypsies); chipboard letters (Zsiage); Misc: Hand Medium fonts

pizza night

2007

Sunday night at the Drumheller household has become Pizza Night, and according to Nate and Daddy - "Mommy's pizza is the best". So the boys pull up a chair and help me make two pizzas, one just pepperoni for them and one pepperoni and sausage for Mommy and Daddy. I think Nate and Zach eat as much pepperoni and cheese as they put on the pizzas, but I don't mind. I love having them help me!

Think Outside the Box

Christine's boys declared Sunday night as "pizza night" and happily joined in on the prep work. When Christine spied this pattern with the funky circles, it reminded her of the boys' favorite topping—pepperoni! She cut that pattern into pizza-shaped circles and mixed it with a few red scraps of patterned paper to highlight the family's Sunday night antics. To add unexpected fun to your own page, choose prints that remind you of details from your story—even if the connection is thinking outside the (pizza) box.

Supplies: Cardstock (Bazzill); patterned paper (7gypsies, BasicGrey, Cross My Heart, Tinkering Ink); letter stickers (American Crafts); mask (Heidi Swapp); sticker (KI Memories); Misc: 2Peas Plain Jane font, ink, paint

Artwork by Christine Drumheller

Linear Analysis

Jenn had a lot of these vertical shots of her daughter in the gym. But it wasn't until she saw the linear designs of the red-and-blue paper that she was inspired to create this fantastic page. Jenn used pieces of the striped pattern both upright and on its side—just like her daughter! Each photo has its own patterned paper mat, but the bold title, large brads and patterned stars tie the design together.

Supplies: Brads, cardstock (Bazzill); patterned paper (Sassafras Lass); chipboard letters (BasicGrey); glitter glue (Ranger); stamp (Stampin' Up); Misc: Myriad Pro font

Artwork by Jenn Olson

Taking Shape

Patterns in paper are great for shaping the details you use on a page. But patterns are also great for inspiring the way your page is actually shaped. Greta noticed the large circle on this snowflake patterned paper, and decided to highlight her photos by placing them within the shape. She added two small strips of pattern down the right side to anchor her embellishments. Placing your title along the curve of your elements adds movement and draws attention to your photos.

Supplies: Cardstock (Bazzill); patterned paper (Creative Imaginations, Dèjá Views); letter stickers (American Crafts); chipboard accents, rub-ons (Dèjá Views); Misc: Batik Regular font

Artwork by Greta Hammond

A Bold Tweetment

On this warm fall day, baby Ella thought a nap was in order. Wouldn't you love to bask in the sunshine? To complement her photos of a sweet sleeping Ella, Kelly chose this "tweet" birdie paper. To add a bold but simple detail, she re-created the bird design and included a ring to mimic the circles on the patterned paper. The handcut details not only add coordinating accents but provide a creative place to house the journaling. Small details like this can take a page from "ho-hum" to "wow!"

Supplies: Cardstock (Bazzill); patterned paper (KI Memories); buttons, letter stickers (American Crafts); chipboard heart (Heidi Grace); decorative scissors (Fiskars)

Artwork by Kelly Purkey

Wake-up Call

I know this green print is anything but restful, but that is exactly why I chose it. The multicolored circles remind me of balls of string, the kind you would tease lazy cats with to get them on their paws! Plus, the zany pattern wakes up the monochromatic color scheme of the photos. The dizzy circles guided my choice of funky letters and the swirly border pattern, as well as the unique title treatment. The cutaway look adds an extra zing to the design.

Supplies: Cardstock (Bazzill, KI Memories); patterned paper (7gypsies, KI Memories); letter stickers (Doodlebug, K&Co., SEI); tab (SEI); paper punches (EK Success); Misc: Arial font

Z&Z

You are cute. You are lazy. You are always hungry, and you love to take naps on the couch. But, we love you because you are ours! Olivia says on 04/04/08

you SNOOZE

Play with it!
Cut out a Title

Materials: Patterned paper, cutting mat, cardstock or patterned paper, adhesive and letters

Identify the spots in your pattern that you are going to cut away from your paper. Choose as many spots as you'll need for your title letters. Cut the elements out using a craft knife.

Place your cut-out pattern over a sheet of solid-colored cardstock or over a contrasting pattern. Attach the sheets.

Add title letters to the spaces cut out from the pattern.

Every year we wish for it. Just a few inches - enough to play in, to sled down the hill, to make a snowman. But, since you were born, we've only had one such snow, and you were too young to remember it. But on March 6th, 2008, 3 days before your 8th birthday, it began falling in huge flakes. We were trying to eat dinner at a restaurant, but you kept running to the door and checking on the progress. I'm surprised you slept at all that night, as the snow continued to fall. Your sister woke you at 6:00AM, so excited herself. And by 7:15, you had convinced me it was time to go outside. Bundling up was another thing you weren't accustomed to, but you were glad I insisted, after you played in the snow for a little bit. And, although my friend in Chicago told me this wasn't snow (she was only teasing me), we thought this snow was {perfect}

Beyond the Obvious

Michaela's outerwear on this snowy day was every color of the rainbow. I converted my photos to black and white to better match the blue-and-green patterns on the page. The funky circle print made me think of snowballs, so I cut them out from the leftover pattern and accented them with swirly rub-on details. When looking to patterns for handcut details, look beyond the obvious to find creative elements to enhance your pages.

Supplies: Cardstock (Bazzill); letter stickers, patterned paper (Chatterbox); brackets, glitter letter stickers, rub-ons (American Crafts); glitter stickers (K&Co.); brads (Doodlebug); Misc: Times New Roman font

3-way Multiple photos, three ways

Here, three different artists use the same photos (above) on a layout. These layouts show that if you let patterned paper be your inspiration, you can successfully highlight multiple photos using different techniques.

She Has a Point

Greta matched these sweet photos with soft pastels in a little boy theme of sailboats, airplanes and stars. Inspired by the diamond shapes in one of the patterned papers, she created a central border with graphic, pointed edges—and accented with red buttons—that divides the focal point photos from the rest of the pictures. The border also serves to highlight Brody in the photos, with its triangular edges pointing directly to him.

Supplies: Cardstock (Bazzill); patterned paper (Dèjá Views, Scenic Route); die-cut shapes, rub-ons (Dèjá Views); buttons (Creative Imaginations); Misc: Batik Regular font

Artwork by Greta Hammond

Back to Nature

The leafy print in this blue patterned paper, which reminded Nicole of the ivy in the photos, inspired a nature theme for the page. So Nicole handcut a leaf from the print to use as an embellishment. She also chose to accent the blue with red, and to handcut wavy designs from another patterned paper to resemble a soft summer breeze.

Supplies: Patterned paper (Creative Imaginations, My Mind's Eye); chipboard letters (American Crafts); vellum cards (Maya Road); button (Autumn Leaves); chipboard accent (Heidi Swapp); Misc: Garamond font

Artwork by Nicole Samuels

Brody is a typical five year old boy...rarely still or in one place for too long! But on our little trip to the park to feed the ducks I was able to sneak a few shots of him. Gotcha, Brody!

GOTCHA!

Tilt-a-Whirl

Brody is a delightful little boy but one who is extremely hard to photograph, as he's never still. After I pulled out papers that matched the red, blues and greens in my photos, one of the patterns in particular guided me in the right direction. The diagonal stripe gave me the idea to tilt my photos. I used that paper to frame the tilted row of photos, placing blocks of it above and below the two pictures.

Supplies: Cardstock (Bazzill); patterned paper (Crate Paper); chipboard number (Zsiage); brads (Imaginisce); rub-ons (Luxe); Misc: Bell MT font

take 5

Brody, you are a typical 5 year old - always on the move, rarely still. But, the deal was, you let me take a few photos for your momma and then we would go to the park, feed the ducks, and ride the carousel. You kept your end of the deal, and we kept ours. Now I've got to come up with something better the next time I want you to take 5 for me!

2007

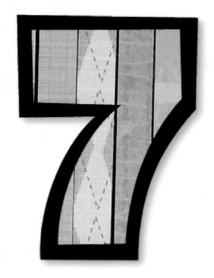

Anything Goes

Using four or more patterns in a variety of ways

By now you've figured out that patterned paper can do just about anything that needs done on a scrapbook page. It can provide the backdrop for your photos. It can be used effectively in small amounts or piled on for layered impact. You can create titles that tease and embellishments that sizzle. You can cover chipboard or use paper to accent your journaling. Paper can be inspiring, and even small scraps can be combined for awesome designs. You can crumple it, cut it, stamp on it, weave it, punch it, distress it, ink it, tear it and piece it. You can mix and match as many colors and patterns as you want. But, most important, patterned paper can enhance your own personal stories and photos. With so many techniques to try and different ways to mix patterns, why not try adding lots of patterns to a page—even four or more!—and see what takes shape. What are you waiting for? Check out this gallery of layouts, then get out there and create. Anything goes!

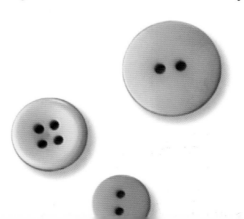

Happiest Page on Earth

Jennifer's family members loved their trip to Disneyland. To commemorate the adventure, she chose bold, bright prints to lend a happy feel to her photos from the park. She balanced the energy in the colors by placing the patterns and photos in a grid on the right. On the left, she balanced her large red background pattern with a bold title treatment. Placing the patterns using a clean-lined design ties the two happy halves together.

Supplies: Cardstock (Prism, Provo Craft); patterned paper (Karen Foster, KI Memories, Scenic Route, Treehouse Memories); buttons, letter stickers (American Crafts); label (Provo Craft); clip, paper punch, tag (Making Memories); floss, ribbon, rub-on letters (Karen Foster); chipboard stars (Heidi Swapp); decorative scissors (Provo Craft); photo corners (Canson); Misc: SP You've Got Mail font

Artwork by Jennifer Gallacher

Stylish Design

I admit to loving all the little appliquéd, painted and embroidered designs found on children's clothing. From whimsical designs to more formal ones, the clothing in your photos can inspire your layout design. These ideas can be re-created with different patterned papers for easy style. Handcut small pieces from paper scraps to create a design, like my sailboat, and attach them to your layout over a simple background pattern.

Supplies: Cardstock (Bazzill); patterned paper (KI Memories, Me & My Big Ideas, Sassafras Lass, Scenic Route); chipboard letters, script word (Heidi Swapp); button (KI Memories); accent word (Li'l Davis); flower (Prima); rub-on (C-Thru); brad (Making Memories); Misc: Berlin Sans FB font

Do you know how hard it is to put a 6 year old in the middle of a field of wildflowers and say "don't pick them"?

Michaela, May, 2006

She actually did really well, but she wasn't crazy about all the bugs who were enjoying the flowers too.

wild flowers

The sign says "don't pick the flowers", or at least that's what it means.

Burst of Sunshine

Set her loose in a field like this and say "Don't pick the flowers"? Yeah, right! I wanted an energetic, springtime feel to play up these photos. With so many patterns, you might worry the photos would get lost, but they don't. The key to this layout is paper colors that are one shade lighter than the colors found in the photos. While busy, the sunny patterns complement the photos. And the lighter background allows the vivid images to burst off the page, like sunshine on a spring day. Experiment with color—go lighter or go darker, but watch the positive effect it has on your photos.

Supplies: Cardstock (Bazzill); patterned paper (Autumn Leaves, K&Co., Making Memories, Pink Paislee); letter stickers (American Crafts, Doodlebug); rub-ons (BasicGrey); chipboard butterflies, rhinestones (K&Co.); Misc: sequins, transparency

I hoped for it, and it came true. Someday, when you have a little one of your own, I know you'll understand. I grew up devouring books. I loved reading, and I was rarely without a book in my backpack, or my purse, or my hands. I would sit down with a book, and look up hours later, wondering how time could fly by so fast. I would take one to bed at night, and read flashlight, or by the light coming thru the crack in my bedroom door. I could ride for hours on a trip without complaining, because my books kept me company. And, you are the same way. And I'm glad, because reading expands your mind in ways that nothing else can. You can take trips, or dream dreams, or have adventures. Books make you think, and imagine, and reach. Books are good friends that you can visit over and over again. So, read, my daughter. Photo, 2007. Journaling, 02/11/08.

you get that from me

READ · my daughter

Winning Combination

If Olivia is quiet, you can most likely find her head in a book. And I was the very same way. To tell the story of our love for reading, I examined my photo and chose a background paper that matched the warm tones behind my subject. Then I pulled out three shades of pink to coordinate with Olivia's shirt, using them to frame her photo. When you find colors that look pleasing to your eye and make your photos stand out, you have a winning combination.

Supplies: Patterned paper (Crate Paper, K&Co.); chipboard letters (Chatterbox); rub-ons (Scenic Route); brads (Doodlebug, K&Co.); epoxy buttons (Making Memories); Misc: Times New Roman font

As you turn into our neighborhood you can't help but notice the beautiful trees growing in our neighbor's yard. During the fall, especially, their colors are vivid and gorgeous. As the reds, yellows, and oranges turn to brown, they fall to the ground, creating a carpet of leaves that any kid would love to play in. You were no exception. Smiling for the camera isn't something you enjoy, but if I'm fast enough, I can capture the real thing, as you dance among the leaves.

Floral Arrangement

As you can see, Olivia would much rather be playing in the leaves than raking and bagging them. For this fall layout, I used an arrangement of several subtle floral patterns the ties everything together. The scalloped border in a dark floral pattern—which contrasts with the light floral damask background—anchors the title and draws attention to the focal photo. To highlight my journaling and ground my photos, I wrapped paper strips in a third pattern around a chipboard frame. Two additional floral patterns, the neutral one behind the journaling and the red one behind the title, accent the page.

Supplies: Cardstock (Prism, Provo Craft); patterned paper (7gypsies); flowers (Prima); rub-ons (Scenic Route); brads (Bazzill); die-cut frame (Sizzix); paper punch (EK Success); Misc: 2Peas Evergreen font

Getting Warmer

Not all photos are easy to scrap, as was the case with these; sharks brought to mind cool blues and grays, but the photos were warm, with lots of brown tones as well as bright aqua. I realized I had no photos of the sharks anyway, and that my story was about my daughter's happiness, so I went to work finding patterns in warm hues. I started with a solid chocolate brown background and built a frame around my photos using scraps of three different papers: subtle patterns in warm brown shades with hints of green and turquoise. I used a fourth pattern in brighter colors to craft dimensional, floral embellishments.

Supplies: Cardstock (Bazzill); patterned paper (BasicGrey, October Afternoon); letter stickers (BasicGrey); chipboard accents, rhinestones (K&Co.); buttons (Autumn Leaves); flowers (Prima); Misc: 2Peas Evergreen font

IT'S EASY BEING GREEN

Everybody seems to be going green these days. Even though you're playing with paper, it doesn't mean you can't get in on the green action. With these ideas, you can help save the planet and create layouts with beautiful patterns, too.

- Use up those scraps!

- Purchase eco-friendly products like those from K&Company.

- Use stamps instead of stickers—you get to use the same image more than once with no leftovers to toss.

- Stick with double-sided paper—twice the options in a single sheet!

- Rather than tossing them in the trash, donate papers you don't want to schools or local charity organizations.

Mat Finish

These photos make me laugh out loud! Despite their funny nature, I went with subtle, soft patterns and colors to complement the brown hair and make the beautiful blue eyes in the photos stand out. I layered four patterns on the page, starting with an almost solid neutral print as the background. For photo mats that are out of the ordinary, layer two subtle patterns under one photo, and place a different, but coordinating, pattern under a second image. Repeat a pattern under your journaling to finish off the layered look. Complete the page with a dressed chipboard accent like the bracket used here.

Supplies: Patterned paper (BasicGrey, Fancy Pants, K&Co., KI Memories, Scenic Route); letter stickers (American Crafts, BasicGrey); glitter chipboard (Making Memories); rub-on (C-Thru); brad (Making Memories); button (Autumn Leaves); chipboard bracket (Fancy Pants)

Accidents Happen

I tried several times to scrapbook these photos, but something about the hot pink in Olivia's shirt kept holding me back. That is, until I unintentionally placed them on top of this soft yellow plaid. The yellow matches the playground equipment in the photos and allows my girl to shine. I added playful color with small pieces of three other patterns, and chose blue buttons and a rub-on arrow for extra pop. You just never know—accidents can turn out to be great designs in disguise.

Supplies: Cardstock (Bazzill); patterned paper (A2Z, Chatterbox, Fancy Pants); letter stickers (Doodlebug, Making Memories); buttons (Autumn Leaves); rub-on (Scenic Route); Misc: Arial Black font

Color My World

Birthdays are joyful and chaotic around our house, and opening gifts is the best part, if you ask Michaela. I wanted to capture that joy in my layout design, so I added a world of bright color accents to the page. For photos that have a lot of action, pattern and/or color like these, use small pieces of patterned paper and surround them with a neutral, solid cardstock "frame." To ensure all the design elements don't swallow up your words, choose a subtle pattern—like this lined—to house your journaling.

Supplies: Cardstock (Bazzill); patterned paper (K&Co., Pink Paislee); letter stickers (Pink Paislee); rub-ons (Creative Imaginations, Scenic Route); felt accents (K&Co.); flowers (Prima); die-cut tags (Adornit); Misc: 2Peas Evergreen font

Soft Spot

I know my girls received their love for stuffed animals from me. This bunny proved to be irresistible, and I love her still after all these years. To showcase these adorable photos, I chose various pastel patterns. Each layer adds a softness and detail to the page. To create a similar look, begin by layering a big piece of "almost solid" (like this pink paper) over a full-size sheet of your busiest pattern. Use two other patterns in single colors—like green-and-white gingham and blue-and-white dots—to create a spot to rest your focal point photo. Choose embellishments in the same pastels to add texture.

Supplies: Cardstock (Prism); patterned paper (Chatterbox, Creative Imaginations, Making Memories, Me & My Big Ideas); letter stickers (BasicGrey, Making Memories); chipboard accents (Making Memories, Me & My Big Ideas); flowers, rhinestone brads (Making Memories); adhesive pearls (K&Co.); buttons (Autumn Leaves); Misc: 2Peas Evergreen font, sequins

Busyness Plan

Little boys have so much energy. To create an energetic layout, I chose bright patterns and accented them with crisp black touches. For unique embellishments, you can layer punched circles with brads, buttons and rub-ons. And using lots of patterns doesn't have to overwhelm your photos. To make sure your photos stand out, use a monochromatic pattern for the background and add photo mats of one or two slightly busier patterns. Save the busiest, most colorful patterns to use as your embellishments.

Supplies: Cardstock (Bazzill); patterned paper, rub-ons (Scenic Route); die-cut letters (QuicKutz); buttons, tags (Making Memories); photo corners (Canson); brads (American Crafts, Making Memories); paper punches (EK Success); Misc: 2Peas Evergreen font

And busy and curious and smart. You are constantly thinking and analyzing and moving. You talk and ask questions non-stop. You've got a smile that is pure magic - flashed quickly and then I only see the back of your head as you are off to explore something else. You are an amazing boy, Brody, and I'm so proud to be your aunt.

Play with it!

Make a Metal Tag Pop

Materials: Metal-rimmed tag (without a white center), craft knife, craft mat, vellum, adhesive and patterned paper

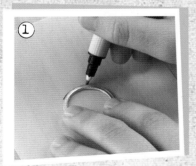

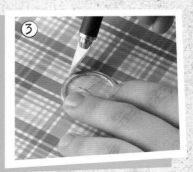

Trace the tag onto a piece of vellum and cut out the vellum circle just inside the line. Add a thin line of adhesive to the back of the metal tag. Attach the tag over the vellum.

Cut a cross in the center of the vellum. Pull back the four triangles. Then add a line of adhesive around the back of the tag and attach it to a piece of patterned paper. Let the adhesive dry.

Cut out the excess paper around the metal tag using the craft knife.

one

two

nine

five

eight

You caught some smaller fish in the pond beside our house, but this is the one that made you smile this BIG smile. And it was bigger than Daddy's catch, which made it even funnier!

how many

fish

Fishing for Complements

I admit, fishing photos plus red and pink might not seem like a great combination. But this fishing layout is meant to be playful and girly, and the red color complements the green. The details are definitely playful, beginning with the handcut fish and the scallop border (created from the "negative" area in the striped photo mat) and ending with the blue patterned wave perfect for a water-themed page. I like how this striped border leads the eyes to the column of photos. For even more pattern, I incorporated blue paper into my fish-shaped title.

Supplies: Cardstock (Bazzill); button, die-cut cardstock (KI Memories); patterned paper (Creative Imaginations, K&Co., Me & My Big Ideas); title font dies (Provo Craft); flower (Prima); rickrack (Maya Road); brads (Doodlebug, Making Memories); rub-ons (Making Memories); Misc: 2Peas Evergreen font

Snow Bold

One look at his face, and you know this little boy's having a ball. To frame her snow-day photos, Amber stitched blocks of patterned papers together. The patterns are bold and used in large pieces, but the photos are bold as well, and the paper colors are similar to those in the photos. Plus, together they communicate icy, cold fun. For a final, clever touch, Amber pieced together a jolly snowman from cardstock and scraps of patterned papers. Notice the lack of other embellishments: A mix of busy patterns can do the job of adding detail all on their own.

Supplies: Cardstock (Bazzill); patterned paper (7gypsies, Chatterbox); clear snowflake (Heidi Swapp); brad (Making Memories); Misc: Times New Roman font, thread

Artwork by Amber Baley

Just Two Good

These photos give you a glimpse of what these two are really like: playful, silly and, sometimes, too rowdy! The funky details in these patterned papers were just what I needed for this silly Christmas layout. I focused on just two papers: The wide piece of funky circles is balanced by the almost solid red pattern in the background. I incorporated small pieces of other patterns as handcut borders and circular embellishments.

Supplies: Cardstock (Bazzill); chipboard and die-cut accents, patterned paper (Scenic Route); holly stickers (EK Success); stamp (Autumn Leaves); brad (Making Memories); Misc: Bradley Hand ITC font

I had an inkling, you see,

I grew up with the best

mother a girl could wish for.

So it's no surprise to me that

she thinks you are

simply the best

grandmother

good times

Around the Block

Cutting patterns into blocks is a no-fail way to design around rectangular photos. Follow my formula for using four patterns successfully in a color-blocked design: Decide on a complementary color scheme, such as red and blue. Then choose two patterns, one dark and one light, in each color. Place your photos on the page as desired, and then add the four pattern blocks to fill the space around the photos. Add a white trim to frame the page. Whether or not red is your main color, adding touches of the happy hue enhances the feeling of love, perfect for a page like this one.

Supplies: Cardstock (Bazzill); chipboard title, epoxy accents, patterned paper (Me & My Big Ideas); Misc: 2Peas Evergreen font

By now you know the drill - if we vacation at the beach, Momma gets an hour of your time and cooperation. And, you have to wear what I want you to wear. And you have to be happy about it. Easy enough, right? But, every year, you ask me "Why do you want to take photos on the beach? Why can't we go to the pool? Why do you think this is fun?" And by the end of the hour (it flies by), you are usually having too much fun to listen to my answers. But someday, honey, you'll have kids of your own, and you'll understand. Someday, you'll be just like me. June, 2006

Someday

Twist and Shout

These are some of my favorite photos, but the story behind them, and not the setting, is the reason for this layout. So rather than go for a beach theme, I opted for a feminine feel with floral embellishments. But I still added lots of blue to represent the ocean setting. I originally stuck with the blue-and-green paper on this page, but it lacked something, despite the torn edges that add dimension to the layers. I realized a twist of color would be just what the page needed. For any page that needs a bit of the unexpected, top a bright pattern on top of black-and-white pieces like I did. Here, little pearl details add a finishing touch.

Supplies: Cardstock (Bazzill); patterned paper (BasicGrey, Making Memories); letter stickers (BasicGrey); pearl stickers (K&Co.); chipboard brackets (Making Memories); Misc: Times New Roman font

WHERE?

Where did time go?

I blinked. Seriously.
And, five and a half years flew by.
You were five, and now you are eleven.

I know time can't really fly, but it definitely
feels like it can. You have the same blue
eyes, and the same thick, sun-streaked hair.

But your smile is different, with your baby teeth
all gone. And, you prefer denim, khaki, and army
green clothes to the sweet florals and pastels.

You still adore playing outside, but you've
traded your swing for a pretend sword (to play
at being a lady knight, of course!)

You no longer play with Grant (he moved away),
but Kole goes exploring with you, and loves games,
swimming, and pretending, just like you.   10/06

Easy as Pie

I've been waiting a long time to scrapbook this photo of Olivia in her denim jacket. When I ran across the older shot of her in our backyard, I knew I wanted to do a "Where did time go?" layout. Playing on the greens and blues in both photos, I pulled three scraps of paper from my scrap box and mixed them with some black-and-cream border stickers across the page. This easy method of combining patterns—choosing pieces that match the photos and slices of patterns in neutrals shades—produced a layout that I love.

Supplies: Cardstock (Bazzill); patterned paper (BasicGrey, Sassafras Lass, SEI); letter stickers (BasicGrey); chipboard accents (American Crafts); stickers (Collage Press); flower (Prima); brad (Doodlebug); Misc: Times New Roman font

3-way One sketch, three ways

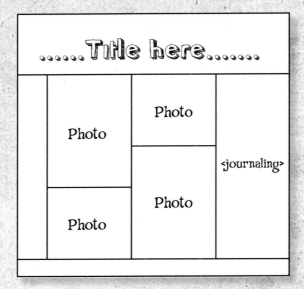

.....Title here.......

Photo	Photo	
		<journaling>
Photo	Photo	

Here, three different artists use the same sketch (above) as the base for a layout. Their layouts show that even with the same sketch as a foundation, anything goes! Four or more patterns can highlight sweet photos in any numbers of ways.

Falling in Love

I found these older photos taken during our first "nature walk" with both of our girls. Although they were printed in black and white, I remember the colors surrounding us as we walked along, so I chose a background print that recalls the colors and textures of that fall day. Another coordinating print contained a flower image, so I cut that out and used it as a large embellishment on the page. The third and fourth patterns—a soothing green and fall-colored stripe—serve as a solid photo mat and ultra-thin border, layered to create a little dimension on the page. Rub-ons, stickers and dimensional accents are a nice complement to this simply designed layout.

Supplies: Cardstock (Bazzill); letter stickers, patterned paper (BasicGrey); rub-ons (BasicGrey, Dèjá Views); Misc: Times New Roman font, button, string

the great outdoors

And so begins our tradition of a fall walk in Tishomingo State Park

together K.K. LiVy DaD

WALK nature

2001 autumn

Six Degrees

Amber combined a whopping six patterns—plus a patterned die cut!—to achieve this look. Yet her photos remain the focus of the page. How did she do that? She applied the almost solid brown to the page as the background to create a place for the eye to rest. Then she used her bold, busy patterns in small amounts. Plus, the colors create a nice contrast to the black-and-white photos. The die-cut tree and scalloped border sandwich her central photo, highlighting rather than hiding it.

Supplies: Cardstock (Bazzill); die-cut letters and shapes, patterned paper, stickers (BasicGrey); buttons (Autumn Leaves); Misc: Susie's Hand font

Artwork by Amber Baley

Oh, Boy!

To highlight the colors in her photos of this adorable baby boy, Susan started with patterns in brown and red. She also mixed several subtle patterns with a high-contrast polka dot one, which also makes the red stand out. The playful dot pattern matches the feel of the baby photos, as well as the little red heart on the bear, while the brown and tan patterns allow the boy to take center stage.

Supplies: Cardstock (Bazzill); patterned paper (BasicGrey, Heidi Grace); die-cut letters (Provo Craft); chipboard sticker, rub-ons (Heidi Grace); paper punches (Fiskars); Misc: Qurillian font

Artwork by Susan Weinroth

Creative Team

As a creative person, **Linda Albrecht** has found so much joy in scrapbooking and papercrafting. She has always loved photos and preserving family history, so her children, heritage and own childhood memories are the reasons why she scrapbooks. Her love for art is the passion that keeps her intrigued with this hobby. Linda loves patterned paper and anything with a worn, vintage appeal. She is so thankful to be a part of such a fulfilling creative outlet that allows her to share with others.
"My favorite paper technique is layering!"

A resident of Wisconsin, **Amber Baley** has been married for 10 years and is a stay-at-home mom to five wonderful children. She has been scrapbooking for 12 years and really enjoys the creative outlet this hobby provides. Amber also enjoy sewing, especially quilting. Once she discovered that she could combine both of her hobbies into one, she dove into scrapbooking and developed a passion for it. Amber had the honor of being a Memory Makers Master in 2006. Her work can been seen in *Memory Makers, Creating Keepsakes, Scrapbooks Etc, Scrapbook Trends* and several other scrapping publications.
"My favorite patterned paper technique is cutting designs out of the patterned paper to highlight the design. I also like to use the paper as inspiration to hand or machine stitch complementing elements."

Christine Drumheller is a stay-at-home mom to two little boys, Nate (seven) and Zach (three); they are a constant source of motivation and inspiration. Before becoming a stay-at-home mom, Christine was a graphic designer. Creativity and art are driving forces and passions in her life; if she does not do something creative each day she gets grumpy—really! Christine has been published in *Memory Makers, Creating Keepsakes* and *Scrapbook Trends* magazines. She was also a 2006 and 2007 Honorable Mention in the Creating Keepsakes Hall of Fame contest. Currently, she is on the design team for Cocoa Daisy and Creative Café.
"My favorite technique? Hands down: mixing patterns! I love to dig through my stash and find unique combinations and ways of blending patterns together."

Davinie Fiero is wife to her local firefighter and mommy to two sweet girls. She is a huge fan of repositionable adhesive and tends to stay up late to get a little scrapping done every day after the kids go to bed. Her work can be seen in most major scrapbooking publications, and she currently designs for Pink Paislee and Studio Calico. Davinie also writes a scrapbooking column for a local parenting magazine and teaches classes at her local scrapbook store.
"My favorite patterned paper technique is to trim out the designs and use them as embellishments."

Irma Gabbard lives in San Diego, California with her husband of 21 years and two children, Ted, who is 19, and Casey, who is 17. She currently is a stay-at-home mom and dog mom to two yorkies and one chocolate lab. Irma has been scrapbooking for nine years and enjoys other hobbies including sewing, cross stitching, home decorating and gardening. She also is an avid snowboarder and surfer.
"My favorite technique is taking my circle punches and punching out circles of patterned paper."

As a designer, writer and teacher in the scrapbooking industry for over 10 years, **Jennifer Gallacher** enjoys the creative process of preserving important memories. As a designer for several companies, Jennifer has enjoyed creating projects for catalogs, Web sites and educational instruction. Jennifer's designs have been published in nearly every major scrapbook and papercrafting publication, and she has received several awards for her work, including Creating Keepsakes Hall of Fame Honorable Mention and Memory Makers Master Runner-Up. You can also see Jennifer's designs on QVC, the Home Shopping Network and Nth Degree (an educational webisode produced by www.creativexpress.com). Jennifer currently resides in Utah with her husband and two children.
"I'm addicted to creating horizontal border strips. I like the way they clearly divide a photo from a journaling block."

Greta Hammond shares her passion for scrapbooking by teaching at her local scrapbook stores and has also had the privilege to work with a number of manufacturers in the industry. She currently designs for Scenic Route, Fancy Pants, Creative Imaginations, Chatterbox and Déjà Views. She was thrilled to have been chosen as a Memory Makers Master in 2007 and inducted into the Creating Keepsakes Hall of Fame in 2006. Greta has been published in numerous magazines and idea books the past several years. She resides with her husband and two children in Northern Indiana. They have been the subject of thousands of photographs and are the main inspiration for her pages.
"My favorite use of patterned paper is to combine pieces to make a pleasing background that supports my photos. I love fitting together different papers to make the most use out of colors, patterns and shapes. It's like a jigsaw puzzle!"

Cari Locken has always loved creating with paper, pens and photos. Preserving memories, special events and everyday moments is one of the many reasosn why she enjoys this form of art. Cari has been scrapbooking for 11 years and has been so blessed by the friendships that this hobby has brought into her life through online scrapbooking sites and design teams. Currently, she is on the design team for *Canadian Scrapbooker* magazine and she enjoys teaching scrapbooking classes at her local scrapbook store and scrapbooking events.

"My favorite patterned paper technique has to be cutting a part of the design from the paper and using that on my layouts."

After scrapbooking for six years, **Mary MacAskill** can't imagine life without this creative outlet. The lives of her family—her husband, Derrick, her daughter, Sadie, and their two pugs, Howie and Owen—are well-documented in her albums, although she is always wishing she had more: more time, more patterned paper and more finished pages! In her previous life, Mary was an environmental engineer, but now she is a very content stay-at-home momma with a penchant for all things paper!

"I absolutely love combining patterned papers from different manufacturers. It just makes me happy when I 'discover' two or three patterns that coordinate in a unique, unplanned combination!"

Jenn Olson lives in Moses Lake, Washington, a little map dot in the middle of the state. She has been married to Eric for nearly 13 years and has three children, Ella (10), Evynn (seven) and Seth (four). Jenn started scrapping in 1997 and has continued in many shapes and forms since then, ending up with a love of paper and digital combined. Jenn stays home with her children and owns her own photography business. She was a Creating Keepsakes Hall of Fame winner in 2006 and has been published in *Creating Keepsakes*, *Simple Scrapbooks* and several online digital publications.

"My favorite patterned paper technique is using one or two really vibrant, striking patterns as accents on an otherwise neutral page."

Kelly Purkey lives in Chicago where there is inspiration (and delicious pizza) around every corner. She is honored to be part of the Creating Keepsakes 2008 Dream Team and designer for Fiskars Brands, American Crafts and twopeasinapucket.com. Besides scrapbooking, she loves traveling, curling up with a good book, laughing with friends and cupcakes with lots of icing.

"My favorite paper technique is using scallop-edge scissors on the edges of paper to add some flair."

Nicole Samuels lives in Williamsburg, Virginia, with her husband and three children. She started scrapbooking about seven years ago, never imagining that this "hobby" would become such a passion as well as a creative outlet from the day-to-day mom duties. Patterned paper is her number-one must-have supply! Nicole's work has been published in *Scrapbooks, Etc.*, *Creating Keepsakes*, *Scrapbook Trends*, *Cards*, and several idea books and online newsletters. She is on the design teams of Pink Paislee, Creative Café and Pageframe Designs. Nicole also teaches scrapbooking and papercrafting classes at her local scrapbook store.

"My favorite technique is to cut out the pattern from the paper and re-design it or refashion it on the layout."

While **Lisa Storms** is a full-time mom by day, she spends her nights in her scrap room with her Diet Dr. Pepper and decorative scissors. Although she created her first scrapbook as the SCA historian in sixth grade, her formal addiction began at a home scrapbooking party in 1998. She is a tool junkie. If it can cut, punch, emboss or otherwise manipulate paper, she must have it. This passion lead her to her dream job as a member of the Fiskars design team, which includes a wide variety of brands such as Heidi Grace Designs, Cloud 9 Design and Li'l Davis Designs. Lisa has been published in numerous scrapbooking and craft magazines, most noteably as a member of Scrapbooks, Etc.'s Creative Team and Creating Keepsakes Hall of Fame.

"I love to find new ways to use patterned paper to create purpose in my designs, and my favorite technique is using unexpected patterns to create paper piecings."

Susan Weinroth started scrapbooking in 2000, and she absolutely loves every aspect of this craft, have made many friends along the way. She is so thankful that it's become such a large part of her life. When she's not crafting, Susan is most likely to be chasing after her one-year-old baby boy, Evan, and their little toy poodle, Toby, too. Susan has been married to her husband, Eric, for seven years, and they currently live in a sunny little community in Ponte Vedra Beach, Florida.

"I absolutely love to put my hundreds of squeeze punches to work—punching shapes and layering them with foam adhesive to create unique embellishments."

Source Guide

The following companies manufacture products featured in this book. Please check your local retailers to find these materials, or go to a company's Web site for the latest product. In addition, we have made every attempt to properly credit the items mentioned in this book. We apologize to any company that we have listed incorrectly, and we would appreciate hearing from you.

7gypsies
(877) 749-7797
www.sevengypsies.com

A2Z Essentials
(419) 663-2869
www.geta2z.com

Adornit/Carolee's Creations
(435) 563-1100
www.adornit.com

American Crafts
(801) 226-0747
www.americancrafts.com

ANW Crestwood
(973) 406-5000
www.anwcrestwood.com

Arctic Frog
www.arcticfrog.com

Autumn Leaves
(800) 588-6707
www.autumnleaves.com

BasicGrey
(801) 544-1116
www.basicgrey.com

Bazzill Basics Paper
(480) 558-8557
www.bazzillbasics.com

Berwick Offray, LLC
(800) 237-9425
www.offray.com

Canson, Inc.
(800) 628-9283
www.canson-us.com

Chatterbox, Inc.
(208) 461-5077
www.chatterboxinc.com

CherryArte
(212) 465-3495
www.cherryarte.com

Cloud 9 Design
(866) 348-5661
www.cloud9design.biz

Collage Press
(435) 676-2039
www.collagepress.com

Crate Paper
(801) 798-8996
www.cratepaper.com

Creative Imaginations
(800) 942-6487
www.cigift.com

Cross-My-Heart-Cards, Inc.
(888) 689-8808
www.crossmyheart.com

C-Thru Ruler Company, The
(800) 243-8419
www.cthruruler.com

Daisy D's Paper Company
(888) 601-8955
www.daisydspaper.com

Darice, Inc.
(866) 432-7423
www.darice.com

Dèjá Views/C-Thru Ruler
(800) 243-0303
www.dejaviews.com

Die Cuts With A View
(801) 224-6766
www.diecutswithaview.com

Doodlebug Design Inc.
(877) 800-9190
www.doodlebug.ws

Dude Designs
www.dudedesignsonline.com

EK Success, Ltd.
www.eksuccess.com

Emagination Crafts, Inc.—no longer in business

Fancy Pants Designs, LLC
(801) 779-3212
www.fancypantsdesigns.com

Fiskars, Inc.
(866) 348-5661
www.fiskars.com

Fontwerks
(604) 942-3105
www.fontwerks.com

Hambly Screenprints
(800) 707-0977
www.hamblyscreenprints.com

Heidi Grace Designs, Inc.
(866) 347-5277
www.heidigrace.com

Heidi Swapp/Advantus Corporation
(904) 482-0092
www.heidiswapp.com

Hero Arts Rubber Stamps, Inc.
(800) 822-4376
www.heroarts.com

Imagination Project, Inc.
(888) 477-6532
www.imaginationproject.com

Imaginisce
(801) 908-8111
www.imaginisce.com

Jenni Bowlin
www.jennibowlin.com

Junkitz
(732) 792-1108
www.junkitz.com

K&Company
(888) 244-2083
www.kandcompany.com

Karen Foster Design
(801) 451-9779
www.karenfosterdesign.com

KI Memories
(972) 243-5595
www.kimemories.com

Li'l Davis Designs
(480) 223-0080
www.lildavisdesigns.com

Luxe Designs
(972) 573-2120
www.luxedesigns.com

Making Memories
(801) 294-0430
www.makingmemories.com

Martha Stewart Crafts
www.marthastewartcrafts.com

Marvy Uchida/ Uchida of America, Corp.
(800) 541-5877
www.uchida.com

May Arts
(800) 442-3950
www.mayarts.com

Maya Road, LLC
(877) 427-7764
www.mayaroad.com

McGill, Inc.
(800) 982-9884
www.mcgillinc.com

Me & My Big Ideas
(949) 583-2065
www.meandmybigideas.com

Melissa Frances/Heart & Home, Inc.
(888) 616-6166
www.melissafrances.com

Mustard Moon
(763) 493-5157
www.mustardmoon.com

My Mind's Eye, Inc.
(800) 665-5116
www.mymindseye.com

October Afternoon
www.octoberafternoon.com

Offray—see Berwick Offray, LLC

One Heart...One Mind, LLC
(888) 414-3690

Paper Company, The - see ANW Crestwood

Paper Relics
www.paperrelics.com

Paper Studio
(480) 557-5700
www.paperstudio.com

Pink Paislee
(816) 729-6124
www.pinkpaislee.com

Prima Marketing, Inc.
(909) 627-5532
www.primamarketinginc.com

Prism Papers
(866) 902-1002
www.prismpapers.com

Provo Craft
(800) 937-7686
www.provocraft.com

Prym Consumer USA, Inc.
www.dritz.com

PSX Design
www.sierra-enterprises.com/psxmain.html

Queen & Co.
(858) 613-7858
www.queenandcompany.com

QuickKutz, Inc.
(888) 702-1146
www.quickutz.com

Ranger Industries, Inc.
(800) 244-2211
www.rangerink.com

Reminisce Papers
(319) 358-9777
www.shopreminisce.com

Sandylion Sticker Designs
(800) 387-4215
www.sandylion.com

Sassafras Lass
(801) 269-1331
www.sassafraslass.com

Scenic Route Paper Co.
(801) 542-8071
www.scenicroutepaper.com

Scrappin' Sports & More
(877) 245-6044
www.scrappinsports.com

SEI, Inc.
(800) 333-3279
www.shopsei.com

Sizzix
(877) 355-4766
www.sizzix.com

Stampin' Up!
(800) 782-6787
www.stampinup.com

Studio Calico
www.studiocalico.com

Target
www.target.com

Technique Tuesday, LLC
(503) 644-4073
www.techniquetuesday.com

Tinkering Ink
(877) 727-2784
www.tinkeringink.com

Treehouse Memories
(801) 318-6505
www.treehousememories.com

Urban Lily
www.urbanlily.com

Westrim Crafts
(800) 727-2727
www.westrimcrafts.com

WorldWin Papers
(888) 834-6455
www.worldwinpapers.com

Wrights Ribbon Accents
(877) 597-4448
www.wrights.com

Zsiage, LLC
(718) 224-1976
www.zsiage.com

Index

Want more ideas for playing with paper?
Check out these other Memory Makers Books!

See what's coming up from Memory Makers Books by checking out our blogs:
www.mycraftivity.com/scrapbooking_papercrafts/blog/
http://www.memorymakersmagazine.com/blog/

601 Great Scrapbook Ideas

Brimming with inspiration and ideas, you'll discover one amazing page after another in this big book of layouts.
ISBN-13: 978-1-59963-017-5
ISBN-10: 1-59963-017-6
paperback
272 pages
Z1640

Organizing Your Scrapbook Supplies

Whether you have a designated scrap room or a coveted seat at the kitchen table, tips from the Memory Makers Masters will get your paper and other supplies organized.
ISBN-13: 978-1-59963-030-4
ISBN-10: 1-59963-030-3
paperback
128 pages
Z2229

Paper Everyday

If you've fallen for the gorgeous patterned paper lining craft-store aisles, you'll love the projects in this book that show you how to put those materials to use in 30 simple and savvy projects to enrich your everyday life.
ISBN-13: 978-1-58180-840-7
ISBN-10: 1-58180-840-2
paperback
128 pages
Z0009

Starting Points

With unique layouts and images of the starting points behind them, you'll be inspired to take favorite photos, memorable notes, trendy new paper and more and use them to fuel fresh layout ideas.
ISBN-13: 978-1-59963-026-7
ISBN-10: 1-59963-026-5
paperback
128 pages
Z2038

These books and other Memory Makers titles are available at your local scrapbook retailer, bookstore or from online suppliers, or visit our Web sites at www.memorymakersmagazine.com or www.mycraftivity.com.